TECHNOLOGY

(5)

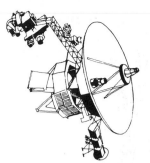

THE MARSHALL CAVENDISH LIBRARY OF SCIENCE
TECHNOLOGY

Marshall Cavendish Corporation
New York   London   Toronto   Sydney

Reference Edition published 1989

©Marshall Cavendish Limited MCMLXXXVI

Published by Marshall Cavendish Corporation
147 West Merrick Road
Freeport
Long Island
NY 11520

Library of Congress Cataloging in Publication Data

The Marshall Cavendish book of technology.
    p.   cm. — (Marshall Cavendish library of science)
    Includes index.
    Summary: Examines the practical applications of science in farming, sports, housework, communications, and other areas.
    ISBN 1-85435-073-0
    1. Technology — Juvenile literature. [1. Technology.]
I. Marshall Cavendish Corporation. II. Series.
T48.M384 1989
600 — dc19

88-28766
CIP
AC

ISBN 1-85435-069-2 (set)

Printed and bound in Italy
by L.E.G.O. Vicenza

CONTENTS

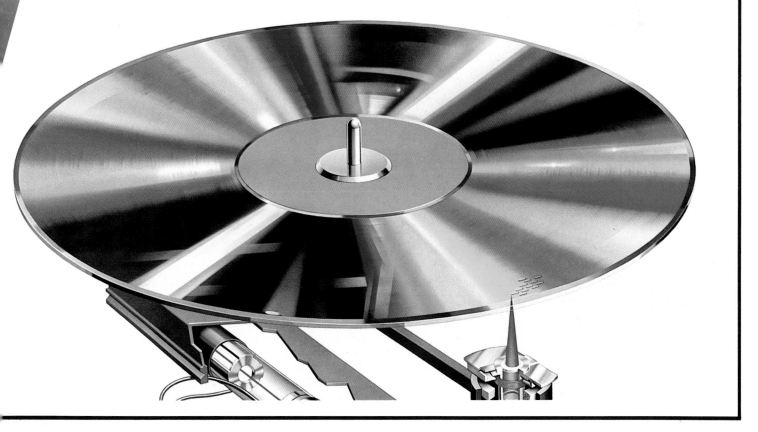

INTRODUCTION

The age we live in is one of the most exciting there has ever been. And it is one that is increasingly dominated by science and technology. Ours is the age of 'instant' communications by telephone and telex all around the world via artificial moons; of lasers that can punch a hole in thick steel plates in a wink of an eye; of supersonic airliners that can travel faster than a rifle bullet; of space telescopes that can spot stars being born in the depths of our galaxy.

But above all, ours is the age of microchips, which are the 'brains' behind our computers. Thinner than a razor blade and small enough to pass through the eye of a needle, microchips carry tens of thousands of electronic circuits that can run an oil refinery; play a Grand Master at chess—and beat him; run your

Below: To develop the oil fields in the deep and treacherous waters of the North Sea, engineers have had to pioneer new technologies in drilling, pipelaying and diving.

Below right: Modern technology demands that we work with dangerous materials, such as radioactive substances. We must handle them remotely with robot hands.

washing machine; or guide the 'hands' of the robot that welds the body panels of your car.

All these modern marvels are the product of technology. Technology puts science to work. It puts theories into practice. It translates chemical equations in laboratories into oil refineries; earthy materials from the ground into metals. It harnesses the energy locked in oil, coal and natural gas, in the wind and waves, to provide power to turn the wheels of industry and to fuel the vehicles that whisk us effortlessly over the land, across the seas and through the air. It shapes the very face of the Earth.

In this book all these and many more aspects of the fascinating world that is technology are vividly revealed and explained in words and pictures.

Below: The components on this printed circuit board are products of the electronics technology that is transforming the way we live and work.

CHAPTER 1

COMMUNI-CATIONS

Radio signals carrying words, pictures and coded messages flash around the world at the speed of light. They are the product of ingenious electronic technology, which has also given birth to the miracle microchip and the computer. Lasers and optical fibres are now being combined in a revolutionary new method of transmitting signals and information that could soon make the copper cable obsolete.

The mammoth dish of an Earth station gathers the faint signals transmitted by spacecraft millions of kilometres/miles away. In turn these signals will be routed to mission controllers via cable and satellite. Such feats of telecommunications are now commonplace.

COMPUTING

It is appropriate that a book about technology should start with computing, because the computer holds the key to our modern world. It would be difficult to find any facet of our lives that is not affected by the computer. Computers help control our factories, forecast our weather, calculate our phone bills, record our bank balance, pay our wages, design our cars, catch our criminals, reserve our airline seats, and so on.

Computers can do so many marvellous things that they seem to be super-intelligent. But they are not intelligent in the usual sense.

In a central control room in Tokyo, computers help engineers check the 17,000 km (10,563 miles) of piping in the city's water supply system, which handles some 5 billion litres (1.1 billion gallons) every day.

The main reason why they appear so superior to human beings is that they carry out their work at an unbelievable speed. The most powerful computers are capable of carrying out hundreds of millions of calculations every second!

Millions of people now own home computers, which can be used both for entertainment, such as playing video games, and for keeping the household accounts. But above all home microcomputers give us 'hands-on' experience of the machine that will influence our lives even more as time goes by. The home computer is called a micro because it has as its 'brain' a microchip, one of the most remarkable products of our age (see page 12).

The microcomputer is the smallest member of the family of computers, which vary in their

capacity to process and store information and in the speed at which they work. Increasingly more powerful than the micro are the minicomputer, used in business and industry, and the mainframe computer, used by large companies, universities and government departments.

All these computers, however, work in a similar manner and have the same basic kinds of equipment. They are all digital computers, which means they handle information and instructions in the form of digits, or numbers. (There is another type of computer called the analog computer, which handles information in analog form.)

HARDWARE AND SOFTWARE

A computer consists of a number of parts that may be separate or

Above: The advent of mass-produced 'micros' has brought computers into the home. Children now start to have 'hands-on' experience at an early age.

Top: Artists can draw colourful computer graphics like this using, not a keyboard, but an electronically sensitive tablet. They draw on the tablet with a special stylus.

It controls the operation of the whole computer and carries out the necessary calculations, acting on data it extracts from a store, or 'memory'. A computer has in fact two kinds of memory. Data needed to run the computer is stored in a permanent read-only memory, or ROM. A temporary random-access memory, or RAM, holds programs and data the computer needs to carry out a particular task.

As mentioned earlier, computers handle all the information and instructions fed to them in the form of digits, or numbers. However, they do not work with decimal numbers, but binary numbers, which use only two digits, 1 and 0. This is because these two digits can readily be represented in electronic circuits by, say, the flow or non-flow of electric current.

Fortunately we do not have to convert all our data and programs into combinations of binary digits, or 'bits'. We instruct the computer in a 'language' of simplified English. Then the computer itself translates this into binary code. Among the common computer languages in use are BASIC and PASCAL.

INPUT/OUTPUT DEVICES

The main method of communicating with a computer is through a keyboard. The keyboard is coupled to a video display unit (VDU), which displays the instructions/information keyed in. Data and programs may be fed into the computer's memory in various ways. It may be by magnetic disk, via a disk-drive unit. The flexible, so-called 'floppy' disk is the most common type. On some micros input is by magnetic tape via a tape recorder. Business computers may also take input by punched cards or tapes, and by various devices that 'read' optical codes (such as the bar codes on goods) and magnetic characters (as on bank cheques).

A permanent visual record is provided by a printer, which in mainframe machines can output at the rate of some 2000 lines a minute!

integrated into a single unit. These form the hardware of the computer. They include the devices used to put information (the 'data') and a set of instructions (a 'program') into the computer and to take results out. The programs are known as the software of the computer.

The main part of the computer is the central processing unit, or CPU.

THE MICROCHIP

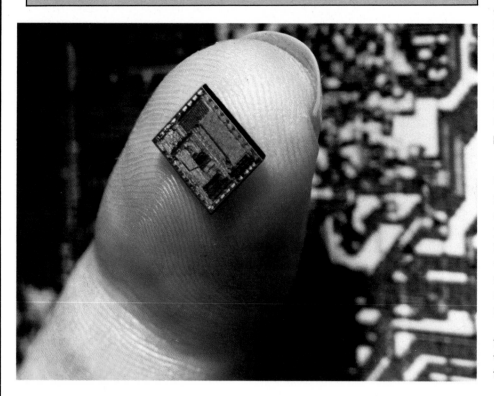

Thin wafers of crystal, made of the most abundant element on Earth, silicon, have begun to revolutionize practically all aspects of our lives. They have made possible such modern wonders as the pocket calculator, the digital watch and the home computer. They are in fact miniature computers themselves. Because they are so small, they can be incorporated in all kinds of machines, large and small, in the home as well as in industry.

These miracle crystal wafers are silicon chips, also called microchips because of their size —they are only a few millimetres square (see above). How do these chips achieve their astonishing feats? They do so because they contain thousands of electronic circuits and tens of thousands of individual electronic components, such as transistors, diodes, resistors and capacitors. These components act together to amplify (strengthen), switch, resist, store and generally manipulate electric currents.

INTEGRATED CIRCUITS

In an ordinary circuit, such as that

Above: The tiny crystal flake that has caused a revolution—the silicon chip. Only a few millimetres square, it holds thousands upon thousands of electronic circuits. Chips like this form the 'brains' of calculators and computers.

Right: This is the electronics module of an electronic typewriter. The machine is controlled by chips, which are mounted in the black rectangular blocks. The chip mounts are wired with other components onto a printed-circuit board.

used in a radio or television set, all the various components are quite large and separate. They are joined together in circuits by wires or thin metal films on a printed-circuit board. The incredible thing about the silicon chip is that all the components and all the circuits are fashioned within a single crystal. They are called integrated circuits.

Integrated circuits represent the latest stage in a process of miniaturization of electronic components that began in 1948. That is the year in which the transistor was invented. The

transistor, made of little chunks of silicon or other semi-conductor material, was then about the size of an aspirin tablet. It did the same job as the standard electronic valve of the time, which was several centimetres in length. In today's integrated circuits the transistors are smaller than a pinprick.

MAKING CHIPS

The silicon chip takes brilliant minds many months to design. Yet once designed, it can be mass-produced in great quantities and therefore cheaply. The first stage of design is to devise electronic circuits that will perform the desired function—as a computer memory device, for example.

Next the method of incorporating the circuits into a chip must be worked out. This involves chemical treatment, or 'doping' of the chip.

By doping the silicon with certain chemicals, its electrical properties can be altered. The various electronic components of the circuits are built up from several layers of differently doped silicon.

For each layer a mask must be placed over the silicon so as to ensure that it is doped only where it should be. The masks are prepared from an illustration of the chip circuits drawn about 250 times life-size, then photographically reduced.

Chips are made several hundred at a time on a disc of pure silicon about 7.5 cm (3 in) in diameter. The first stage of chip-making is to heat the disc in a steam oven. This

Right: A designer works on the electronic circuitry of a chip, using a diagram magnified many hundreds of times. When complete, the diagram is photographically reduced to form a mask for doping the silicon.

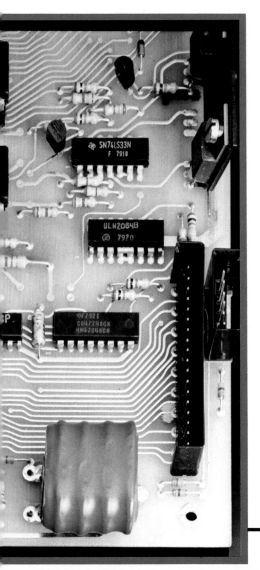

oxidizes the silicon surface. Then the disc is given a light-sensitive coating and the first mask is put down. It is exposed to light, which shines through the mask in certain areas and affects the coating there. Solvents remove the exposed areas of coating, leaving the oxide layer showing through. The disc is next treated with acid. This etches, or bites into and removes, the exposed areas of oxide. This bares the silicon there. The rest of the oxide layer which is protected by the coating, is unaffected. Next the coating is removed and the chip is placed in a doping oven and exposed to a chemical vapour such as phosphorus. The chemical diffuses into the exposed base silicon and changes its properties.

For the complete chip, as many as 12 stages of masking, etching and doping are required. In a final stage a thin film of aluminium is deposited to connect the various components to external circuits.

After manufacture, the disc of chips is examined and tested by an automatic probe. A diamond cutter then slices up the disc into individual chips. Afterwards they are mounted on an insulating base and connected by fine gold wire to tiny pads that are linked with pins that fit into an external circuit board.

Fact file . . .

The most advanced memory chips have the capacity for storing over 1 megabit (one million bits) of information.

A microprocessor chip about 9 mm (0.35 in) square has the same computing power as a room-full of computer equipment of 20 years ago.

RADIO AND TV

The air all around us is full of invisible magnetic and electrical vibrations that carry words, music and pictures. These vibrations are radio waves. We cannot detect them ourselves, but our radio and TV sets can, and translate them into sounds and images that entertain, inform and educate.

The radio revolution began in experiments carried out by the Italian Guglielmo Marconi in the 1890s. He invented what was then called wireless telegraphy— sending messages from point to point without using wires to carry them. In the first decade of this century, the wireless began carrying voices, and the radio was born. Regular radio broadcasting, however, did not begin until the 1920s. The same decade also saw the infancy of television. John Logie Baird demonstrated a workable system using mechanical picture scanning in 1926.

CARRIER WAVES

A radio broadcast begins when sounds enter a microphone in a studio or elsewhere. The microphone changes the pattern of incoming sound waves into varying electrical signals. As they are, the signals can pass along wires but they can't travel through the air. So they have to be combined with a radio wave, which *can* travel through the air. The process of combining the sound signals and radio carrier wave is called modulation.

After amplification, the modulated wave is broadcast from the transmitting aerial. The aerial of a radio receiver picks up the wave, amplifies it and then

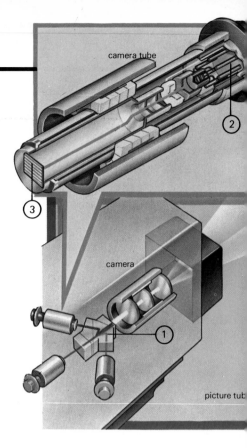

separates the audio signals from the carrier wave. This process is called demodulation, or detection. When the audio signals are passed to a loudspeaker, the original sounds that entered the microphone are reproduced.

Many radio programmes are broadcast simultaneously on carrier waves of different wavelengths. You select the one you want by tuning—adjusting the electronic circuits of your receiver so that they pass just one wavelength. The wavelengths vary from thousands of metres (long wave), hundreds of metres (medium wave), metres (short wave) and fractions of metres (VHF). VHF stands for 'very high frequencies'.

PICTURE SIGNALS

Television programmes are also transmitted through the air on radio carrier waves. This time the waves carry two sets of signals—audio (sound) and video (picture). The sound is converted into audio signals by a microphone, as before. The pictures are converted into video signals inside the television camera. It is simplest if we consider first the transmission of a black-and-white picture.

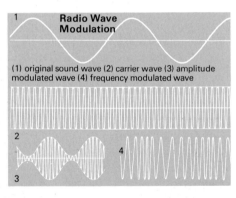

Radio Wave Modulation

(1) original sound wave (2) carrier wave (3) amplitude modulated wave (4) frequency modulated wave

Left: The two ways in which a radio wave can be modulated, or altered for transmission through the air; (3) amplitude modulation and (4) frequency modulation.

Below: A transmitter sends out a modulated radio wave, which 'carries' sound signals. The receiver sorts out these signals and feeds them to a loudspeaker.

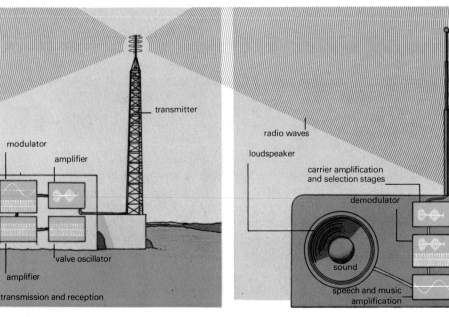

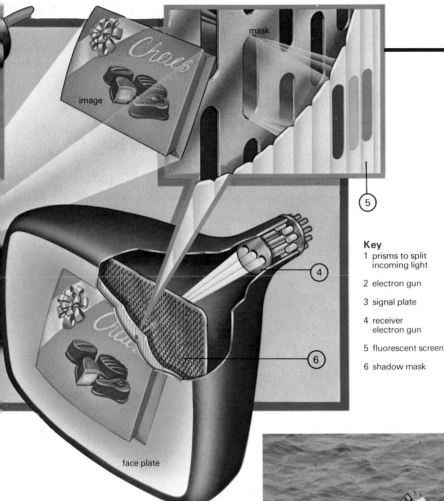

Key
1 prisms to split incoming light

2 electron gun

3 signal plate

4 receiver electron gun

5 fluorescent screen

6 shadow mask

Left: A look inside the television camera and the picture tube. Inside the camera special prisms split up the incoming light into the three primary colours — blue, red and green. Three camera tubes convert this light into electronic signals which are transmitted. The signals eventually reach the picture tube of the receiver. There, an electron gun 'fires' three beams representing blue, red and green, and recreates a true colour image on a fluorescent screen.

Below: Using a portable camera and recording equipment, television newsmen cover a lifeboat rescue exercise. Portable video cameras and recorders are now widely available to the public at large.

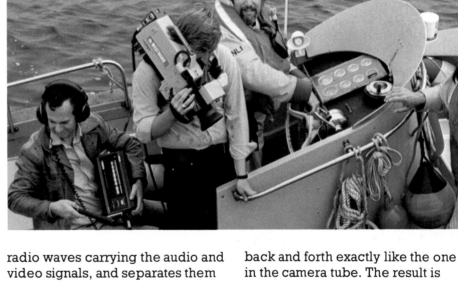

Inside the TV camera the pattern of light representing the scene viewed is focused by a lens onto an electronic tube. It falls on a plate where the pattern of light is converted into a pattern of electrical charges. The plate is then bombarded by a beam of electrons from an electron 'gun'. The beam moves rhythmically over the plate from left to right and from top to bottom in a series of lines (in Britain 625 lines). This is called scanning.

The strength of the beam of electrons reflected back from the plate depends on the amount of charge the plate carries at any point, which represents the amount of light at that point in the original scene. This reflected beam thus holds the picture signals, which are then combined with the radio carrier wave and broadcast.

For colour transmission a camera uses three camera tubes, which separate out the patterns of red, blue and green light in the scene viewed.

A television receiver picks up the radio waves carrying the audio and video signals, and separates them out. The audio signals go to a loudspeaker, the video signals to the picture tube, properly called a cathode-ray tube. The video signals are fed to an electron gun in the narrow part of the tube, which emits a beam of electrons that varies in strength like the reflected beam from the camera tube. The electron beam travels to a fluorescent screen.

Meanwhile, scanning signals are fed to magnetic coils around the tube which make the beam scan back and forth exactly like the one in the camera tube. The result is a re-creation, line by line, of the pattern of light that originally entered the camera tube. The lines merge to form a picture.

For a colour picture, three electron guns carrying signals for red, blue and green fire beams at the screen, where they light up phosphors of the appropriate colours. The colours merge to form a true colour picture. A so-called shadow mask ensures that each beam hits only phosphors of the right colour.

These days it is easy to pick up the telephone and call someone in another country, or another continent. The telephone system carries your voice through wires, maybe through glass fibres, on radio waves, and often through space to its destination hundreds or even thousands of kilometres away. Telephoning is the most common form of long-distance communications, or telecommunications. But there are many others, such as telex, facsimile, electronic mail, and viewdata (see page 19).

Samuel Morse began long-distance communications in the 1830s when he began sending telegraph messages along wires, using a simple code of dots and dashes. In 1876 Alexander Graham Bell produced the first crude telephone, allowing voice to be transmitted. Ten years earlier telegraph messages had been sent across, or rather under, the Atlantic Ocean by cable. But a transatlantic telephone service did not begin until 1927; calls were made by radio telephone and were at the mercy of fluctuating atmospheric conditions.

A transatlantic telephone cable laid in 1956 improved matters, while six years later the satellite Telstar showed the way ahead by relaying telephone calls and TV programmes from space. Today communications satellites are a key link in all intercontinental telecommunications systems. The latest Intelsat satellites can handle 15,000 telephone conversations, as well as two colour TV channels, at the same time.

THE TELEPHONE

Modern telephones are a far cry from Bell's original model and even from the ones available a decade ago. They vary in shape and features. They have push buttons instead of dials and memories to store telephone numbers. Some are cordless—the handset is not attached to the base unit, but is linked to it by short-range radio.

However, the principles of telephony have remained the same from the beginning. The telephone handset has a mouthpiece containing a microphone, and an earpiece containing a receiver. When you speak into the mouthpiece, the sound waves vibrate the diaphragm of a microphone containing carbon grains. The vibrations cause the grains to be more or less compressed, which alters the strength of an electric current passing through them. This results in electrical waves that vary according to the sound waves of your voice.

The electrical waves travel along the telephone lines to the person you are calling, and enter the receiver in the earpiece. There they make the magnetism of an electromagnet vary, which causes a metal diaphragm to be attracted more or less. In other words the diaphragm vibrates, and in so doing it makes sounds. These sounds create a replica of your voice.

Almost everywhere, you get through to the person you wish to call by dialling a number. Each number contains a code that identifies the region (and country if it is an international call) where that person lives. Dialling the number sends a series of pulses along the telephone lines.

These pulses activate a sequence of switches in the telephone exchange, which route your call through to the person you want. The older exchanges use electromagnetic switchgear, which is noisy and slow. New models use rapid and silent electronic switching.

In fact the whole telephone network is going electronic now. In an electronic network the voice

Right: This is a modern Telex machine, which can store incoming messages in its memory while the operator is working at the keyboard.

Left: This experimental home videophone system is being tested in West Germany. It uses optical-fibre cables to carry the telephone and television signals. When operational, the system will also carry TV channels, teletext and radio programmes.

Below: This apparatus is used for the intricate process of joining together the optical fibres (inset) in telecommunications networks. Such fibres transmit signals as coded laser pulses.

signals are no longer carried by electrical waves, but as coded electronic pulses. The pulses are coded in digital, binary code.

The pulse-code signals can be sent at high speed, not only through the copper cables of the ordinary telephone network, but also through optical fibres. Then they are first converted into pulses of laser light. Optical fibres, made from ultrapure glass, are as fine as human hair but can carry thousands of telephone calls at the same time. Fibre-optic cables have hundreds of times the capacity of copper cables, and are replacing them.

WORDS AND PICTURES

There is a modern equivalent of the telegraph pioneered by Morse last century. It is telex. Telex is a system of sending written messages over telecommunications links. When you type a message on the teleprinter, the words are coded into electrical pulses. They travel over the telex lines to the teleprinter of the person you are calling, and make that teleprinter type out the message you typed.

Pictures, too, can be transmitted via the telecommunications links, by facsimile (or fax) machines. They have a device that scans the pictures and converts the pattern of reflected light into electrical signals, which are then transmitted. In the receiving machine, the signals go to a printer, which recreates the original picture.

Among the latest developments in sending written messages is electronic mail. A letter typed on a special terminal, or a word processor or a microcomputer with a suitable adaptor, can be sent over standard telecommunications links and received on a similar machine. British Telecom operates such a system, called teletex. Other electronic mail systems have the electronic equivalent of a mailbox. Subscribers to the system tap into a central computer and leave messages addressed to other subscribers in its memory.

These days the television set can do much more than just entertain and bring news. It can be a source of almost limitless information. Suitably adapted, it can tap into networks that specialize in providing a wide variety of information, from the local weather forecast and traffic news to the current share prices on the stock market and the departure times of international airline flights.

The general name for information services that you can pick up on your television is Videotex. There are two basic systems, one called teletext and the other called viewdata. Teletext is transmitted along with the ordinary television broadcasting signals. Viewdata comes via the telephone network.

Britain pioneered both videotex systems. The British Broadcasting Corporation (BBC) began transmitting its teletext system, called Ceefax ('See facts') in 1976. The British Post Office, now British Telecom, began the first viewdata service, called Prestel, three years later.

TELETEXT

The teletext signals are transmitted in code in spare scanning lines at the top of the ordinary television picture. To decode the signals and display the information on your screen, you need to have an electronic decoder fitted. This converts the signals into words and graphics—simple pictures.

If you have a teletext set, you access the information using a keypad, which may well be incorporated with the remote-control device for changing channels. The pad will have a

'Text' key, which will bring the information display 'pages' to the screen when pressed.

The first image, or 'page' that comes up on the screen is an index, which directs you to the pages you require. You will be referred to a three-figure number, which you then key on the pad. The page you want will not appear at once. You can see the page numbers changing at the top of the screen. When the page you selected comes up, it will be displayed and held.

Because of the waiting time involved, the teletext system cannot have too many pages. People would lost patience if they had to

Right: A page from the viewdata system Prestel. Many thousands of pages of information on a variety of subjects are available from the central computer data bank.

Below: This is a special terminal used by subscribers on the French viewdata network called Teletel. It enables the subscribers to buy goods from shops using a credit card (inserted in the bottom left-hand corner) without leaving home.

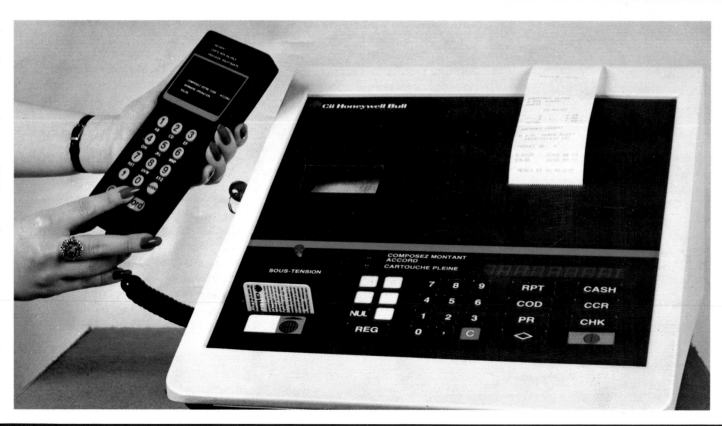

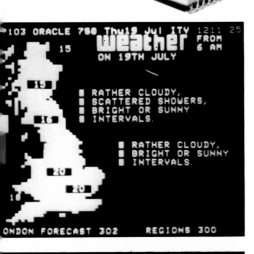

Above: This is a purpose-built viewdata terminal. Users are connected into the viewdata network by the telephone. They call up the pages they require by pressing the page numbers on the key pad.

Left: These are two pages from the teletext system Oracle, produced by Britain's Independent Broadcasting Authority (IBA). In this system the pages are transmitted in code along with the ordinary television signals.

wait more than a few seconds. So 300 pages or so is about the limit.

VIEWDATA

By comparison the viewdata system offers a virtually unlimited number of pages. The Prestel network, for example, already has over a quarter of a million! As mentioned earlier viewdata information comes to you via the telephone lines. When your set is connected into the system, the lines connect you to a computer with a massive memory store.

Again, your television set must be specially adapted. Then you can call up the index and key in the

pages you require via a keyboard, as before. Unlike teletext, viewdata is not a free service, however. You must pay for the time you are on the telephone and for the computer time you take up. Some of the pages supplied are free.

Viewdata is one of the most exciting developments of the video age. It can be used not only to tap into the memory banks of the controlling computer, but to tap into those of other computers. Prestel, for example, has a system, appropriately called Gateway, which provides the path to other computer memory banks.

More importantly, viewdata can be an interactive, or two-way communications system because signals can be sent both ways along telephone lines. Using this facility, people in some areas can now practise home banking. Their bank gives them a code which gives them access to details of their account in the bank's computers. They can then pay bills or transfer money into other accounts, in or out of banking hours.

Soon it will be possible to shop from home in a similar way.

RECORDING

The prolific inventor Thomas Alva Edison began it all in 1877 when he received a 'Halloo' back from a contraption he called a phonograph. He began marketing his machine, which was the first record player. It reproduced sounds when a needle (stylus) was placed in the grooves of a recording in much the same way as the modern record player does. But his recording took the form of a rotating cylinder covered with tinfoil. Today an ordinary record is a plastic disc rotating on a turntable.

When magnified, the grooves in a record disc are seen to have wavy sides. The waves represent the recorded sound. When the stylus of the record-player pick-up passes along the grooves, it is made to vibrate. The vibrations pass to a crystal or another device and are translated into electrical signals. The signals are amplified and then fed to a loudspeaker.

The record disc is a copy of a master disc made in a recording studio. In the studio, sound waves enter the recording microphone which changes them into corresponding electrical signals. These signals are made to vibrate a stylus, which cuts a wavy groove in a lacquered disc. This disc is then used to make a master, from which the commercial discs are pressed.

COMPACT DISCS

The ordinary record discs are usually classed as 'singles' or 'LPs'.

The latest type of disc, however, is much smaller, produces far superior sound reproduction, and is played back in a totally different way. It is the compact disc, which is only about 12 cm (4.7 in) in diameter. It is played back by means of a laser beam.

The reason why the compact disc gives such superior reproduction is that the sounds are recorded on it in the form of a precise digital code. In the recording process, the microphone signals are converted into a series of numbers so that each part of the signal has a precise value. And it is this series of numbers that is recorded, in the binary code, which uses just 0s and 1s. These digits are recorded physically on the disc as a series of microscopic pits and flats. The laser beam 'reads' the code on the record, which is then converted back to signals that are fed to the loudspeaker.

Above right: Musicians performing inside a recording studio. In the foreground the sound engineer works at the sound mixing console. He uses it to control the quality and balance of the recording.

Below: Compact discs like this offer much better sound reproduction than ordinary record discs. Only 12 cm (4.7 inches) in diameter, they play for up to an hour.

TAPE RECORDING

More popular than the record player now as a means of reproducing sound is the cassette tape recorder. This plays a tape about 4 mm (0.16 in) wide which is permanently wound on spools inside a plastic cassette. Professional tape-recording equipment still uses wider tape

on open reels, which has to be threaded from one reel to the other through the recording head.

The tape for all recorders is basically the same. It is a plastic ribbon which carries a coating of magnetic material, usually iron oxide or chromium oxide. When recording, the tape passes over a recording head. This is a kind of electromagnet to which the signals from the recording microphone are fed. They cause its magnetism to vary, and this variation creates a pattern in the magnetic coating on the tape. When playing back, the magnetic pattern on the tape causes the magnetism of a playback head to vary. And this sets up signals similar to those that came from the microphone. When these are fed to a loudspeaker, the original sounds are reproduced.

Picture signals from a TV set or a video camera can also be recorded on tape, called videotape. It is much wider than ordinary sound-recording tape—typically some 50 mm (2 in) wide, and for home use is contained in a cassette. The playback head of the videotape recorder zig-zags from side to side across the moving tape to pick up the signals.

video disc

lens assembly

tangential mirror

prism

the VLP laser

The videodisc records pictures as well as sounds and plays them back through a television set. The disc is 'played' by a laser beam. This is reflected by the record as it rotates. The reflected beam is converted into electronic signals, which are then fed to the TV picture tube.

grating

photo-sensitive diode

lens

PRINTING

Johannes Gutenberg began the printing revolution more than 530 years ago.

Gutenberg's method of printing, called letterpress, using raised metal type, was used for most printing purposes until a few decades ago. But all that has now changed. Most printing now is done by offset-lithography (litho).

Most type is now set, not in metal, but electronically on computerized machines. The typesetter works at a keyboard and videoscreen. As he types the words of the copy to be set, they appear on the screen. They then go into the machine's memory and are stored on magnetic disc or tape. From the disc or tape they can be displayed on paper or printed on film. The printing plates are made from the film.

OFFSET-LITHO

The printing plate for the offset-litho method of printing is made by a photographic technique. For plate-making, negative film is used, in which the type areas are transparent and the rest is opaque. In the process the film is laid on a

Photocopying is an 'instant' printing technique that produces copies in seconds. On this Xerox machine light is reflected from the document onto a selenium-coated drum and produces an electrical image there. The image attracts ink powder (toner) which is then transferred to paper. The heated rollers fuse the powder to fix the final image.

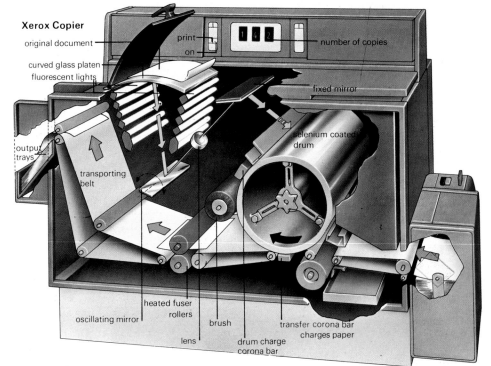

Xerox Copier
original document
print on
number of copies
curved glass platen
fluorescent lights
fixed mirror
output trays
selenium coated drum
transporting belt
heated fuser rollers
oscillating mirror
brush
transfer corona bar charges paper
lens
drum charge corona bar

Below left: The three main printing processes. Lithography, or litho, prints from a flat printing plate; letterpress from a raised plate; and gravure from a recessed plate.

Below: Chip-controlled electronic typewriters like this are rapidly replacing electric machines in the home as well as in the office. They may have fewer than 100 moving parts.

flat image

Lithography

raised image

Letterpress

recessed image

Gravure

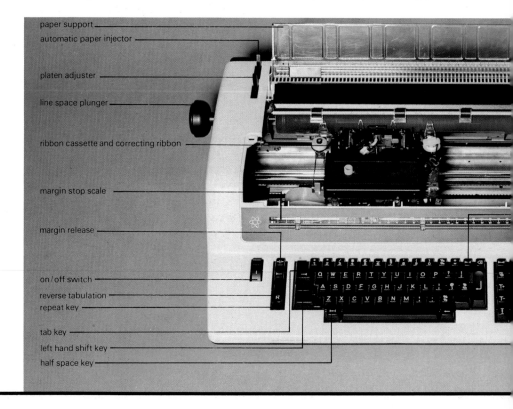

paper support
automatic paper injector
platen adjuster
line space plunger
ribbon cassette and correcting ribbon
margin stop scale
margin release
on/off switch
reverse tabulation
repeat key
tab key
left hand shift key
half space key

All aspects of printing have been revolutionized by new technology. Here layout artists design magazines on computer video display units, manipulating images in the computer memory.

NEW TECHNOLOGY

Even newspaper publishing, long resistant to change, is converting to the new technology. Reporters, for example, use word processors to prepare their copy. The words they type are displayed on a videoscreen, where they can be corrected. They then go into the memory. They can then be transferred to the videoscreen of an editor for correction, and finally sent to a typesetting machine.

The editors can also layout the pages of the paper on the screen using the copy in the memory banks. The pages can then be set complete on film.

metal plate having a photosensitive coating. Light is then shone through it, and after processing, an image of the type remains on the plate. This image has the property of attracting ink and repelling water.

On the litho printing machine the plate is wrapped around a cylinder, which is wetted and inked in turn. So the ink only sticks to the type areas. The printing cylinder transfers, or offsets the image to

another cylinder ('blanket'). This in turn passes the image to the paper, which is wrapped around the impression cylinder.

IN FULL COLOUR

Electronic methods are also used now to prepare the illustrations for litho printing. Colour illustrations are prepared by a process called colour separation. The method is based upon the principle that any colour can be produced from a combination of red, blue and green light. So in colour separation the redness, blueness, and greenness in a picture are separated by means of colour filters. The results are four pieces of film, representing the three colours and black.

The printer makes printing plates of these separations. When he comes to print, he inks the plates in yellow, magenta and cyan. When these colours combine, they reproduce the original colours.

Right: The ingenious Microwriter is a kind of cross between a typewriter and a word processor. You press different combinations of the keys for each letter of the alphabet. They appear in the liquid crystal display (LCD) window above and are at the same time stored in the Microwriter's memory.

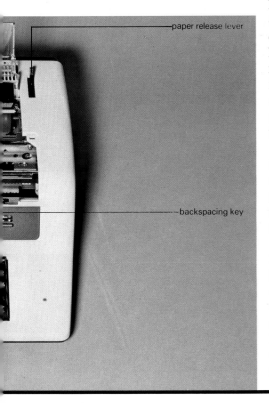

paper release lever

backspacing key

microwriter

PHOTOGRAPHY

When certain silver salts, such as iodide and chloride, are exposed to light, they are invisibly changed. They carry a latent, or hidden image of the pattern of light that fell on them. By chemical processing, this image can be revealed. This is the simple principle behind one of the world's most effective communications medium—photography.

The modern camera is a marvellous precision instrument which now offers almost 'idiot-proof' photography. Electronic eyes, microchip brains and infra-red or sonar beams work together to more or less guarantee success.

In essence a camera is a light-tight box, with a lens and shutter at one end and light-sensitive film at the other. The shutter is opened for a fraction of a second and the lens focuses the light coming in from the scene outside onto the film. The film is a strip of transparent cellulose acetate, covered in an emulsion containing silver salts. The emulsion invisibly records the pattern of light that falls on it.

To bring that image to light, the film is processed, or developed. It is treated (in the dark of course) with a developer, a chemical that changes the light-affected silver salts into metallic silver. The unaffected salts are then washed

Many of the latest cameras rely heavily on electronics for their operation. Electronic circuits containing microchips work their automatic focusing and automatic exposure systems.

away, a process known as fixing. The result is a negative image—the film appears darker where most light fell on it, that is, where the scene was brighter. A positive image is obtained by printing. Light is passed through the negative onto another piece of film, and then that is developed. The tones of the negative are thereby reversed and the true pattern obtained.

Colour films have a number of layers of emulsions that record respectively the amounts of blue, green and red the incoming light contains. The film is then developed, and the image in each layer is replaced with a colour dye. The colours merge to give a true colour picture.

THE SINGLE-LENS REFLEX

The most popular camera used today is the 35-mm single lens reflex (SLR); 35-mm refers to the width of the film. In a SLR camera, light enters the lens and is reflected by a mirror and then a prism into the viewfinder. When a picture is

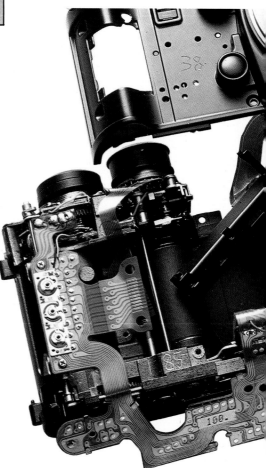

Below: Three stills from a film made using time-lapse photography. It shows stages in the growth of a plant. The plant is photographed at intervals of, say, 15 minutes, over a period of days. The sequence is then played back at normal speed. The plant can then be seen growing—a process usually invisible to the naked eye.

The light path through the SX-70 camera

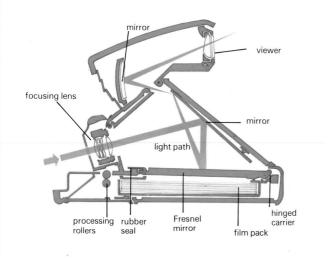

taken, the mirror flips up and allows light onto the film.

The SLR typically has an interchangeable lens, which can move in and out for focusing, and an aperture (opening) that is adjustable. It has a shutter that can operate at different speeds, which allows exposure of the film for different periods of time, typically from about 1/500th of a second to 1 second. The fast speeds are used to 'freeze' movement.

The photographer adjusts the aperture and shutter speed so as to allow the optimum amount of light onto the film. This varies with the lighting conditions and the film speed. Many cameras now have a built-in light meter that helps the photographer choose the correct aperture and shutter speed.

There are many other kinds of cameras. Disc cameras are very flat and take their pictures on a disc film. Compact 35-mm cameras feature a fixed lens and often autoexposure, built-in flash (when lighting is poor), autowind (winding on the film automatically), and automatic focusing.

Other larger single-lens reflex cameras take roll film rather than cassettes, including the world's finest camera, the Hasselblad. And the film is wider, at 55 mm (2¼ in). This film is also used in twin-lens reflex cameras, which have separate lenses for viewing and picture taking. 'Instant' cameras like the Polaroid take their pictures on film that develops itself. It contains 'pods' of chemicals that get to work when the film is ejected from the camera after the picture is taken. Ultra-high speed cameras use ingenious devices such as rotating prisms and mirrors to freeze action that happens in tens of thousandths and even millionths of a second.

A picture produced by holography, a kind of photography that can reproduce images in three-dimensions (3D). The images are formed on photographic film by means of a laser beam. The film is developed to form a hologram, which contains 3D information about the object photographed. Some holograms show meaningless patterns and only produce 3D images when laser light is shone through them. Others produce images when white light is reflected from them.

CHAPTER 2
TRANSPORT

In only a century the 'horseless carriage' has come to dominate our lives, dealing a near-deadly blow to the train. But the railways are fighting back with superfast trains that can often beat many planes for intercity travel. Evolving technologies are making planes more economical, and lifting boats out of the water to avoid the great drawback of water transport—drag. In space flight, however, air drag is harnessed to slow down returning spacecraft like the space shuttle.

With its body leaning into the curve of the track, Italy's Pendolino train need not slacken speed as it goes round bends. This helps it maintain a high average speed on existing railway tracks.

This experimental concept car features extensive computer control.

1 three beam headlights
2 electronic display panel
3 power assisted steering
4 computer controlled driving position
5, 9 radar sensors
6 automated windscreen wipers
7 coded entry button
8 anti-skid brakes

It has been a little over a century since the motor car, or automobile, was born. Late in 1885 German engineer Karl Benz fitted a petrol engine to a three-wheeled vehicle to create the first motor car. Fellow-countryman Gottlieb Daimler independently produced a four-wheeled vehicle a few months later.

However, not until 1908 did the age of the motor car really begin. In that year Henry Ford started mass-producing the famous Model T on an assembly line. He literally put America on wheels, which changed the way of life there for ever. America is still regarded as the 'home of the automobile' and has more cars than any other country. It has about 160 million out of a world total of some 420 million.

SMALL IS BEAUTIFUL

Until the mid-1970s petrol, or gasoline, was relatively cheap, particularly in the United States, which has abundant supplies of oil. Then came a dramatic increase in the price of oil, which set car manufacturers looking for ways to improve petrol consumption. In general they reduced the size and weight of their cars and made the engines more efficient. Today many engines are controlled electronically to keep them always at their best. Further economy is achieved by streamlining car

bodies. This cuts down air resistance, or drag, which absorbs a lot of energy.

'Gas guzzling', or high consumption of fuel, is not the only thing for which the car has increasingly come under attack. Another is pollution. When petrol is burned in the engine, poisonous fumes are given out in the exhaust, particularly carbon monoxide and lead compounds. The fumes can also get trapped in the lower atmosphere in certain weather conditions and cause a deadly smog. Los Angeles is particularly noted for this.

So legislation has been passed to force motor manufacturers to reduce the exhaust emission from their vehicles. This may be done by improved engine designs or by passing the exhaust gases through units called catalytic converters. The problem with the latter is that it increases fuel consumption. To reduce the amount of lead in the air, many engines have been modified to run on lead-free petrol.

THE PETROL ENGINE

An increasing number of cars are now being fitted with diesel engines (page 30). They are longer lasting than petrol engines and their fuel consumption is much better. Experimental electric, steam and

even hot-air engined cars are also under development. But for many years to come the petrol engine will remain the prime power source for cars.

The petrol engine has more than 150 moving parts. It is one of the most complicated machines we ordinarily come into contact with. But of course we expect it never to let us down! The main parts of the engine are the pistons, which move up and down in cylinders, and a crankshaft which the pistons force round. They are contained in a heavy cast-iron engine block. The turning motion of the crankshaft is carried by the car's transmission system to the driving wheels. Most engines have their cylinders arranged in-line, or in a row, but some have two lines of cylinders arranged in a V-shape. Most in-line engines have four or six cylinders. A V-eight cylinder engine is popular in higher power cars.

Petrol vapour is burned in a combustion chamber at the top of each cylinder by an electric spark. The hot gases produced force the piston down to turn the crankshaft. A regular cycle of operations takes place in the cylinders, known as the

Right: Car manufacturers deliberately crash cars to test the safety of their designs and to see the effect of the crashes on dummy passengers.

TRANSMISSION AND DRIVE

A car's transmission system transmits the drive from the crankshaft to the driving wheels. In the usual arrangement the engine is at the front of the car and drives the rear wheels. But many cars now have front-wheel drive: a front engine drives the front wheels. And some cars have four-wheel drive, in which the engine drives both the front and the rear wheels. This kind of drive gives excellent roadholding and is beneficial in icy weather or other hazardous conditions.

four-stroke cycle. In turn the petrol vapour is drawn in as the piston moves down (stroke 1); compressed as the piston moves up (stroke 2); ignites, expands and forces the piston down to produce power (stroke 3); and forced out as the piston moves up again (stroke 4).

Above: A video display unit is an unusual feature of this dashboard of the experimental car shown opposite. It can display TV channels and a range of data.

Right: Track racing demands a very different car design. High power and good road-holding are vital as well as superb brakes!

ENGINE SYSTEMS

The fuel system supplies petrol to the engine. In most cars it is turned into vapour as it is mixed with air in a carburettor. But many now have fuel-injection: petrol is injected directly into the cylinders. A similar system is used on diesel engines, where diesel fuel is injected in the same way. The spark to ignite the petrol comes from the ignition system. This uses an ignition coil, a kind of transformer, to boost the low-voltage (12 volts) current from a battery to more than 15,000 volts.

The burning fuel gives out a great deal of heat, which is removed by the cooling system. A few engines are air-cooled, but most are water-cooled. Anti-freeze is added to the coolant to prevent it from freezing in winter. The heat is removed by water circulating through the engine block. Some heat is also removed by the lubrication system, although its major function is to keep the moving parts well oiled, and prevent rapid wear.

Whatever the drive, all cars have a gearbox to alter the drive-wheel speeds in relation to the engine speed. Cars with a manual gearbox also have a clutch, a device that disconnects the engine from the gearbox when the driver wants to change gear. Cars with automatic transmission have a clutch and gearbox that operate automatically.

In rear-wheel drive, a propeller shaft carries the motion to the rear wheels. Front-wheel drive cars need no such shaft. The propeller shaft is linked to a complicated set of gears (the final drive) in the middle of the rear axle. They turn the motion through a right-angle to drive the wheels, and also allow each wheel to travel at a different speed around corners.

TRUCKS & TRACTORS

On and off the road trucks, or lorries are the real workhorses among our motor vehicles. They transport virtually anything: bricks and rocks, containers and concrete, milk and meat. The trucks used to carry these goods all have different bodies to suit their load.

Bricks are ordinarily carried in a drop-side truck, named because one side hinges down for easy removal of the load, often by fork-lift truck. Rocks are carried by dumper truck, a rugged off-the-road vehicle with the high-sided body, emptied by a hydraulic ram mechanism that tips it up. Some dumper trucks are truly gigantic. General Motors Terex Titan can carry a colossal 318 tonnes!

Container trucks carry goods loaded in standard-sized containers. The truck body is flat, and the container is loaded onto it by specialist handling equipment. Containers are usually 6 or 12 metres (20 or 40 ft) long and 2.4 metres (8 ft) square in section. There is container-handling equipment available at certain rail terminals and ports to allow rapid transfer of containers between truck, rail wagon and ship.

Concrete, milk and meat trucks also have their special features. Freshly made liquid concrete is transported in mixer trucks, which have a conical body rather like a cement mixer. It is rotated all the time to prevent the concrete setting. Milk is carried in bulk in a cylindrical tanker body; meat in an enclosed refrigerated box-like body.

TRUCK DESIGN

The trucks mentioned above all seem quite different, but in fact they are basically quite similar. They have a similar kind of engine and basic framework on which is built a special body. This also holds true for other commercial vehicles, such as buses, fire-engines and dustcarts.

The basic frame, or chassis of a truck is made up of welded steel, girder-like sections that give great rigidity. The chassis is mounted on the wheel axles by springs, usually leaf springs. In the smaller trucks two axles are normal, at front and rear. Larger trucks often have three or even four axles. This gives the truck better traction, or pulling power. In a typical four-axle design, both front axles will be used for steering and both rear axles carry the drive.

Some of the lighter trucks may have an ordinary petrol engine to power them, but most trucks use a diesel engine. Named after its inventor, Rudolf Diesel, this engine is tougher and longer-lasting than the petrol engine, and uses a light oil as fuel. It is a piston engine that is like a petrol engine in many ways. Its pistons move in cylinders in a four-stroke cycle and turn a crankshaft that transmits power. And it is also cooled and lubricated like a petrol engine.

COMPRESSION-IGNITION

However, there is a major difference between the two kinds of engine in the way the fuel is burned. Diesel fuel is burned by what is called compression-ignition, not by a spark. The four-stroke cycle of the diesel engine is somewhat different from that of the petrol engine.

On the first downstroke of the piston, air (not fuel mixture) is drawn into the engine cylinders. On the next upstroke, air is compressed to three times the pressure it is in the petrol engine. This compression makes the air

This bus drives along the railway tracks. But it can be converted in minutes back to a road vehicle. For rail travel the bus is fitted with a retractable guide wheel (inset).

The auxiliary, or splitter box may have two or three speeds.

TRACTOR-TRAILERS

Many trucks these days are formed of two distinct units, an engine or tractor unit, and a trailer. The truck tractor typically has a four-wheel shortened frame, with a so-called 'fifth wheel' on top which can slip under the front of the trailer and latch onto a kind of turntable coupling there. The coupling is flexible, allowing tractor and trailer to swivel independently.

This gives what is called an articulated truck. It allows great flexibility in operation, since tractors can serve a number of trailers at any time.

very hot. Fuel is then injected into the cylinders, where it is immediately ignited by the heat of the air. The gases produced expand and drive down the piston. The power of the engine can be increased by turbocharging. More air is forced into the cylinders by a turbine driven by the exhaust gases escaping from the engine.

To make it easier to haul heavy loads, trucks generally have a gearbox with more speeds than an ordinary car. Many indeed have two gearboxes. The main gearbox would typically have about five or six gears, or speeds, but may exceptionally have as many as ten.

Below: This modern tractor features four-wheel drive and extended wheels with twin tyres on each for better grip. Unusually it is the rear wheels that swivel for steering.

Above: A rugged dumper truck hauls a heavy load of broken rock in a quarry. It has four-wheel drive and is articulated for greater manoeuvrability.

Below: A bus being tested on a tilt table to see how stable it is.

The Ford Four-Wheel Drive Tractor

1	insulated cab	7	axles
2	air conditioning	8	battery
3	diesel engine	9	transfer case
4	instrumentation	10	drive shaft
5	gear selectors	11	hitch
6	transmission	12	high traction tyres

TRAINS

Right: This experimental Japanese train travels a few centimetres above the track. It is levitated, or lifted into the air by magnetic forces.

Left: The 'Red Devil', a steam loco still in use in South Africa. Steam locos are also in widespread use in Asia and South America.

At the beginning of the 19th century, one or two engineers began building steam engines that ran on rails to haul mine wagons. In 1825 one of them, George Stephenson, built a railway that also hauled passenger wagons, the Stockton and Darlington Railway. After he had built the Liverpool and Manchester Railway five years later, 'railway fever' gripped the world.

From then until the late 1940s, trains were the main form of long-distance transport overland. Then they went into serious decline as more and more people turned to cars and planes. But in many countries the decline has stopped and passengers are being attracted back to the railways which are cleaner, faster and more economical than ever before. Today the trains are no longer hauled by the lovable, but terribly inefficient and dirty steam locomotives of Stephenson's era. They are hauled by diesel, electric and even gas-turbine locomotives, which are as efficient as they are clean.

DIESEL LOCOS

Diesel locomotives use the same kind of engine as trucks do, the diesel engine. It is an internal combustion engine that runs on a light oil (see page 30). Locomotive diesel engines, however, have many times the power of truck engines. Also they are turbocharged, which means that air is blown into the cylinders by a powerful rotating fan that is itself powered by the exhaust gases from the engine.

Most diesel locomotives are diesel-electrics. This means that the engine power is transmitted to the driving wheels via an electric generator and motors. The diesel engine runs at a constant and highly-efficient speed and drives the generator to make electricity, then the electricity is fed to electric motors that turn the driving wheels.

There are two other types of diesels in use. Diesel-hydraulic locomotives, particularly favoured in Germany, use a hydraulic coupling between the engine and the drive shaft to the wheels. This oil-filled coupling, called a torque converter, is similar to that used in the automatic transmission of cars. Diesel-mechanical locomotives have a transmission similar to that used on trucks. They are generally small units used for shunting (switching) duties and for passenger work on low-density lines.

ELECTRIC LOCOS

Electric locomotives have a lot going for them. They are relatively simple machines. They have rapid acceleration and can travel at high speeds. Also they are quiet and cause no pollution whatsoever. Their great disadvantage is that they can only run on specially equipped and expensive-to-build track, from which they take their power. Diesels, of course, can run anywhere.

Most electric locomotives pick up their power from an overhead wire, or conductor. Contact is made through a hinged arm, or pantograph on top of the locomotive. The overhead-wire system often operates at 25,000 volts AC (alternating current).

Some countries have electric locomotives that pick up electricity from a so-called third rail. This is a rail laid alongside the usual pair. A metal shoe on the locomotive slides along this rail and picks up the current. The Southern Region of British Rail has quite an extensive third-rail network. The London Underground is also a third-rail system.

SUPERTRAINS

In Japan and France run the fastest trains around. Japan introduced a super-fast rail network as long ago as 1964, when its famous Shinkansen (New Trunk Line) opened.

The Shinkansen is specially built straight and level, rather like a rail motorway. Along the track run the famous 'bullet trains', named for their severely streamlined shape. They regularly reach speeds of

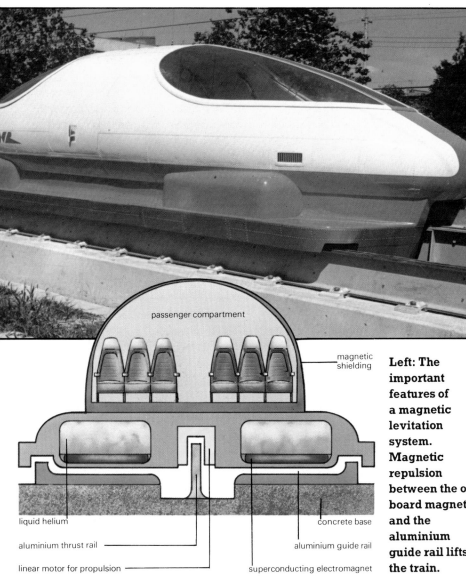

over 200 km/h (125 mph).

The fastest speeds, however, are regularly achieved by France's streamlined TGVs (Trains à Grande Vitesse). They also run on specially built track, between Paris and Lyons. The TGVs can cover the 400 km (250 miles) between the two cities in about two hours. They often touch speeds of over 250 km/h (156 mph).

MAGNETIC LEVITATION

Rail speeds nearly double those of the TGV may be commonplace in tomorrow's world. But the locomotives and trains will not run on ordinary track because they will have no wheels! Instead they will glide a few centimetres above the track, kept aloft by magnetic forces. This kind of system is called maglev, short for 'magnetic levitation'. The diagram left shows the sort of hardware that will be used in the future. Experimental maglev vehicles have already achieved astonishing speeds in recent tests.

passenger compartment

magnetic shielding

liquid helium

aluminium thrust rail

linear motor for propulsion

concrete base

aluminium guide rail

superconducting electromagnet

Left: The important features of a magnetic levitation system. Magnetic repulsion between the on-board magnet and the aluminium guide rail lifts the train.

Below: One of France's TGVs (*Trains à Grande Vitesse*), which provide a superfast service between Paris and Lyons. Electrically powered, they run on specially built straight track.

SHIPS

Ships have been crossing the oceans carrying the bulk of the world's cargo almost since the beginning of civilization. They have also down the ages played a vital role in warfare, as they still do. There is great variety among modern ships: trawlers and other fishing boats; tugs and harbour dredgers; freighters and ferries; container ships and ore carriers; cruise liners and tankers. Each of these types of vessels has a different design that suits it for its particular role on the high seas.

Currently some of the largest ships afloat are oil tankers. Biggest ship of all is the 458-metre (1504-ft) long tanker *Seawise Giant*. She (ships are always female) has a beam (width) of nearly 69 metres (226 ft) and a deadweight tonnage (cargo capacity) of nearly 565,000 tonnes. Other giants among ships are liners such as the 315-metre (1035-ft) long *Norway* (once called the *France*) and the 323-metre (1092-ft) long American aircraft carriers of the Nimitz class.

THE SUPERSTRUCTURE

In general you can recognize a particular kind of ship by its superstructure, or the kind of structure built above the hull. Easiest to spot is the tanker, whose superstructure is sparse, consisting of a unit containing the funnels, bridge and crew accommodation. It is usually located aft—at the rear of the vessel. Most of the deck is clear. The aircraft carrier is also unmistakable, with again only a tiny superstructure. The built-out deck is broad and flat. In the Nimitz class of carriers it occupies an area of no less than 1.8 hectares (4.5 acres)!

Freighters that carry general cargo have only a little more superstructure but carry numerous derricks, simple cranes for loading and unloading cargo. In container ships the cargo is carried on and below decks packed in standard-sized boxes, or containers, making for easier handling. Cruise liners and ferries have the most extensive superstructure, which provides accommodation for the passengers, as well as shops, restaurants etc.

SHIPBUILDING

Practically all ships these days are

**Below: Ferries are among the toughest ships afloat, operating in all but the severest weather conditions. They are sturdily built and have engines at the bows as well as at the stern.
Inset: One of the control consoles on the bridge of a cross-Channel ferry.**

constructed from steel. Steel plates form the hull, the horizontal decks and the vertical bulkheads, the three main types of structure that make up the ship. Mostly these days the plates are joined together by welding, which makes for a stronger and lighter construction than the older process of riveting.

All ships are now driven by screw propellers located at the stern (rear). Some ships, such as ferries, often have additional propellers forward to help manoeuvring. Two main types of engine are used in ships for driving the propellers— steam turbines and diesels. Diesel engines power smaller vessels, such as trawlers and ferries. They are larger versions of the engines that are used to power trucks (see page 30).

The large ships, such as liners and tankers, use steam turbines. They deliver an incredible amount of power. The twin turbines of the liner *Queen Elizabeth 2*, for example, develop more than 100,000 horsepower! Mostly the boilers that raise the steam for the turbines are fired by furnaces burning oil. A few ships, however, have nuclear power units, in which nuclear reactors provide the heat for the boilers. The Nimitz class of aircraft carriers are nuclear powered, as are several Russian icebreakers, such as the 25,000-tonne *Rossiya*, launched in 1983.

Smaller naval vessels are often constructed from GRP (glass re-inforced plastic) that is cheaper and lighter in construction, resists detection by magnetic mines and has a low radar signature. These vessels are often powered by aircraft-derived gas turbine engines.

Top right: The aircraft carrier USS *Enterprise*. Practically all the deck area is given over to runway space for the planes to take off and land. Middle right: Sails are used on this tanker, the *Shin Aitoku Maru*, to provide additional power. They are controlled by computer.

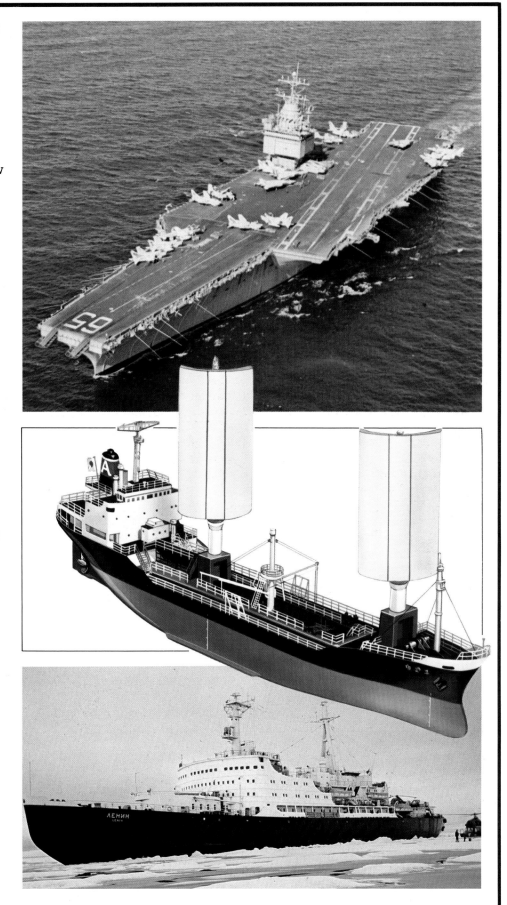

Above: Russia operates a fleet of powerful icebreakers to keep her northern shipping lanes open in winter. Some are nuclear-powered.

SURFACE SKIMMERS

Ships are by far the slowest means of transport we have. Whereas airliners cruise at speeds of up to about 950 km/h (600 mph) and ordinary saloon cars can exceed 160 km/h (100 mph), ocean liners can scarcely manage 30 knots (55 km/h, 35 mph). Indeed most ships travel much more slowly. The thing that holds ships back is the drag, or resistance of the water.

However, there are two kinds of vessels that overcome this problem, each in different ways. They tend to skim over the surface of the sea, rather than sail in it. The vessels are the hydrofoil boat and hovercraft. Hydrofoil boats can travel at speeds double those of ordinary ships. Hovercraft are capable of travelling even faster.

Other surface-skimming craft include so-called ram-wing, or ground-effect aircraft. They are sometimes called aerofoil boats. They have a broad, boat-like hull and wide wings angled upwards. They fly close to the surface of the water, and build up before them a kind of air cushion. This cushion helps support the craft, which means that they don't use as much power for lift as a normal plane does.

HYDROFOIL BOATS

When a hydrofoil boat is stationary in the water, it looks just like any other vessel. But when it starts moving, a strange thing happens. As it gets faster, it starts rising up out of the water! Eventually the whole hull lifts out. All that remains in contact with the water are struts front and rear and a shaft down to the propeller. Because the hull is now out of contact with the water, it experiences much less drag, and the boat can travel very much faster.

What makes the hull lift out of the water? The answer is underwater 'wings'. The struts act as, or are attached to surfaces that act as underwater wings. These wings, or hydrofoils, hold up the hull just like a plane's wings, or aerofoils, hold up the plane. When the hydrofoil moves through the water, it develops 'lift'. When it is moving fast enough, this lift is high enough to support the boat above the surface.

There are two main types of hydrofoils, illustrated in the top and bottom pictures on these pages. The vessel at the top has what are called surface-piercing foils shaped like a shallow V. The one at the bottom has submerged foils. The struts lead down to horizontal foils.

Most hydrofoil boats have surface-piercing foils, which are a more stable design. But passengers tend to get a rough ride in rough water. Boats with submerged foils are less affected by waves, but require a better control system to keep them stable.

Both designs, however, have one thing in common. They kick up very little spray and have a very small

Above: This swift hydrofoil boat operates in the Greek Islands. Built in Russia, it has hydrofoils of the V-shape, surface-piercing design, which can make the ride rather rough in bad weather conditions.

Right: One of the most successful hovercraft designs, the SRN Super 4 car ferry, which operates across the English Channel.

Below: The Boeing Jetfoil is the world's most advanced hydrofoil boat. It uses computers to incline its submerged foils at the correct angle.

Fact file . . .
Telephone inventor Alexander Graham Bell built a hydrofoil boat in 1918 which achieved a speed of 115 km/h (72 mph).

British engineer Christopher Cockerell first demonstrated the principle of the hovercraft in 1955, using a vacuum cleaner and an assortment of tin cans.

'wash', making them ideal for inland waterways.

THE JETFOIL

The boat with submerged foils illustrated here has a sophisticated control system, masterminded by computer. It is the most advanced hydrofoil boat in service around the world, called the Boeing Jetfoil. It has twin gas-turbine engines, but is actually propelled by twin water jets, hence its name.

Water is drawn in through an inlet in the rear foil unit. The gas turbines drive pumps that force the water out through twin nozzles in high pressure jets.

HOVERCRAFT

The hovercraft skims over the surface of the water (or indeed land) in an entirely different way. It glides along on an air cushion. It is one kind of air-cushion vehicle, or ACV. The world's largest hovercraft, the SRN4, ply as car ferries across the English Channel, travelling at speeds up to 65 knots (120 km/h, 75 mph). Some 56 metres (185 ft) long, they have a beam (width) of 28 metres (92 ft) and can carry up to 418 passengers and 60 cars. The main drawbacks with hovercraft are that they are very noisy and create a lot of spray. But passengers seem willing to put up with this for a speedy sea crossing.

The hovercraft may be considered as much an aircraft as a boat since it is propelled by air propellers. But they face backwards, unlike a plane's propellers. The craft may be steered by swivelling the propellers themselves or by deflecting the propeller airstream by means of air rudders. They have powerful fans to create a cushion of air beneath them. Sea-going hovercraft have a rubber 'skirt' around their lower edge that drops down to the surface. This prevents the air from leaking away too quickly.

The bigger hovercraft are powered by gas turbine or diesel engines. The SRN4, for example, has four gas turbines, each of which drives a propeller and fan. By contrast the AP1-88 hovercraft is powered by four diesels. Two drive the twin ducted propellers, while two drive the lift fans.

A hovercraft has several big advantages over ordinary land or sea craft. Firstly, it is both these things at the same time, and therefore able to cross the sea and run right up onto the beach without stopping. It can travel across land on any reasonably flat surface, over swamps or through waterways blocked with reeds, ice or other obstructions. It can even travel upstream against rapids.

SUBMERSIBLES

The most deadly warships in the world do not sail on the high seas but under them. They are submarines. The latest ones are nuclear powered and are able to remain underwater for months at a time, virtually undetectable from the surface. And they carry nuclear missiles with an awesome destructive capability.

The United States and Russia both have a fleet of submarines like this. Russia's Typhoon-class vessels, for example, are some 170 metres (560 ft) long and carry 20 long-range ballistic missiles with a total of 140 nuclear warheads. The similar-sized American Ohio class submarines carry 24 Trident missiles, each with 12 nuclear warheads.

SUBMARINE PRINCIPLES

Submarines may vary in shape and method of propulsion, but they use the same basic principles for diving, staying underwater and surfacing. They are constructed with a double hull. The space in between forms so-called ballast tanks, which are open to the sea. Water in the ballast tanks can be emptied by forcing in compressed air. In this way the weight of the vessel can be varied.

On the surface the ballast tanks are kept empty, or rather filled with air. To dive, the air is let out, allowing water in, and the submarine sinks. Surfacing is the reverse operation. Compressed air is used to 'blow' the water from the ballast tanks. Underwater, the water in the ballast tanks is adjusted so that at any depth, the submarine neither sinks nor rises. It is in a state of neutral buoyancy.

DIFFERENT DESIGNS

There are two main types of submarines—conventional and nuclear. Conventional submarines generally are cigar-shaped and have a speed of less than 30 knots (about 55 km/h or 35 mph). Nuclear submarines on the other hand have a more bulbous, teardrop shaped hull, which provides better streamlining. As a result they are capable of much higher underwater speeds than conventional ones. Russia's Alpha-class vessels are reported to have a top speed perhaps as high as 45 knots (over 80 km/h, 50 mph).

Both types of submarines have much in common, however. They have an oval conning tower, or 'sail', which projects above the hull. It provides the bridge for navigating on the surface. It houses the periscope and radio antennae and snorkel, which is a tube for taking in air while the rest of the vessel is still below the surface.

At the rear of the submarine is the screw propeller that propels it. Just forward of the propeller is a cross-shaped arrangement of vertical and horizontal fins with movable sections at the rear. These form the rudder (vertical fins) and aft diving planes (horizontal fins). There is

another pair of movable diving planes, also called hydroplanes, near the bows (front). The diving planes are angled as necessary during ascent and descent.

SUBMARINE PROPULSION

On the surface conventional submarines use a diesel engine to propel them. Underwater they use electric motors, powered by batteries. They cannot remain submerged for too long because the batteries have to be recharged, on the surface by the diesel engine. In a war situation, this need to surface regularly makes them vulnerable to attack.

Nuclear submarines are propelled by steam turbines. The steam is raised using heat from a pressurized-water nuclear reactor. This is a particularly compact type of reactor. The great advantage of nuclear propulsion is that the submarine does not have to keep coming to the surface to charge its batteries. Indeed it can stay submerged for months at a time.

SUBMERSIBLES

Many miniature submarines are now used commercially to support diving operations, notably in the offshore-oil industry. These vessels, called submersibles, are powered by electric motors and generally have a crew of one or two. They are often equipped with manipulator arms, floodlights, cameras and closed-circuit TV. They operate down to several hundred metres.

Some act as transport to ferry divers to and from their place of work on the seabed. Called lockout submersibles, they have a separate compartment that can be pressurized to match the external pressure of the sea.

Fact file . . .

The United States built the first nuclear submarine, *Nautilus*, in 1955. In 10 years, travelling 530,000 km (330,000 miles) she used only 5 kg (11 lb) of uranium fuel.

The deep-diving submersible, the bathyscaphe *Trieste*, in 1960 descended 11 km (6.8 miles) into the Pacific.

Right: The Polaris submarines carry 16 nuclear missiles, housed in 'silos'. The picture shows the silos with all hatches open.

AEROPLANE DESIGN

People began flying 200 years ago in balloons, which are lighter-than-air craft. But the aircraft age did not really begin until they fathomed the secrets of heavier-than-air flight. The English scientist George Cayley was perhaps the first to work things out in the early 1800s. And in 1804 he built a glider that could fly. But not for 99 years did a powered aircraft take to the skies for the first time.

This happened on 17 December 1903 at Kitty Hawk in North Carolina. On that day a flimsy contraption built of wood, cloth and wire, and powered by a petrol engine left the ground for just 12 seconds. Named *Flyer*, it was the brainchild of the Wright brothers Orville and Wilbur.

Flyer travelled just 36 metres (120 ft) on its historic first flight. This is only a little over half the length of today's most popular long-distance airliner the Boeing 747 'jumbo jet'!

Just about everything in aviation has changed since those pioneering days. Planes are now built with aluminium, a lightweight metal which was virtually unknown in the Wright's day. The engines that power planes now burn kerosene (paraffin) not petrol, and they work on quite a different principle. They no longer spin a propeller for propulsion, they instead derive their thrust from a jet of high-speed gases.

BACK TO BASICS

However, the things that haven't changed over the years are the principles on which heavier-than-air flight depends. The key to flight lies in the shape of a plane's wings. They have a special cross-sectional shape which is broad at the front and sharp at the rear; curved on top and flat underneath. This shape is known as an aerofoil or airfoil.

When an aerofoil moves through

Right: This Grumman X-29 research plane shows the shape of things to come. It features a forward-swept wing.

Right: A design for a supersonic plane being tested in a wind tunnel. Unusually it has its engines arranged in pairs, one above and one below the wings.

Below: Testing of a model of the highly manoeuvrable aircraft technology (HiMAT) vehicle developed by NASA.

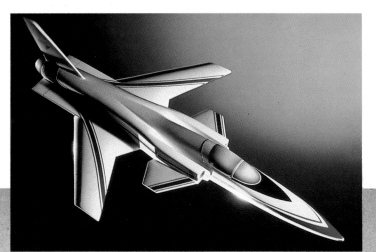

One of the world's fastest jets, the Lockheed SR-71 *Black Bird*. It can travel at speeds of over 3000 km/h (2000 mph).

GOING SUPERSONIC

The wings of planes that travel at supersonic speeds (those greater than the speed of sound) must be highly swept back. The plane must also have a long sharp nose, and its whole body must be carefully shaped. This is so that it can travel supersonically without creating too many shock waves. Many supersonic planes, like the SR-71 pictured above, have a triangular, or delta wing. So does the Anglo-French Concorde airliner, which travels at Mach 2, or twice the speed of sound.

At these speeds the design of the engine air intakes is critical. The shape of the whole intake and the angle of the intake ramp is often changed automatically depending on the speed of the aircraft.

The problem with delta or highly swept back wings is that they cannot travel slowly. So planes that want to travel relatively slowly as well as fast have variable-geometry wings. The wings extend nearly at right-angles for take-off and landing for low-speed flight. Then they can be swept back for high-speed flight. The American General Dynamics F-111 is a swing-wing design like this; so is the European Panavia Tornado.

Some new kinds of planes being tested have even odder wing designs. NASA's Ames-Dryden Flight Facility is testing a design in which the wing is swept forwards not back (see inset picture opposite). It has also designed an oblique-wing plane, in which the wing is straight at take-off, then pivots so that one half sweeps forward and the other back.

the air, the air flows faster over the curved top than along the flat bottom because it has farther to go. By a well-known scientific law called Bernoulli's principle, the faster air flows, the lower is its pressure. This means that the pressure above an aerofoil is lower than that beneath, so that it tends to lift upwards.

So this is how a plane can take to the air. Its engine drives it along the runway faster and faster. The faster it travels through the air, the more its aerofoil wings tend to lift. When the lifting force acting upwards is greater than the plane's weight acting downwards, the plane will rise into the air and start to fly.

WINGS AND TAIL

All planes have wings; a body, or fuselage; and a tail. The wings provide the lift; the fuselage provides space for passengers or cargo; and the tail helps to steady

the plane, like the feathers of an arrow keep its flight straight. The tail has a vertical part called the tail fin or vertical stabilizer, and a horizontal part, called the tailplane, or horizontal stabilizer.

The pilot controls the plane in the air by means of hinged surfaces at the rear of the wings and tail. He tips the wings by means of ailerons near the ends (one up, one down). He puts the nose up or down by moving the elevators at the rear of the tailplane, and turns the plane to right or left by means of the rudder on the tail fin.

The shape of a plane's wings largely depend on the speed at which the plane flies. Low-speed planes, like the Lockheed Hercules transport (550 km/h, 340 mph cruising speed), have their wings almost at right-angles to the fuselage. At the speeds of a modern airliner like the Boeing 767 (850 km/h, 530 mph), the wings must be swept back.

FLIGHT OPERATIONS

As a visit to an airshow or an airport will reveal, there is enormous variety among the aircraft flying today. The ones that thrill are the superfast supersonic fighters and interceptors, sleek as darts, armed to the teeth, and capable of speeds maybe as high as three times the speed of sound—beyond 3000 km/h (2000 mph). But the ordinary traveller will be most familiar with subsonic airliners, travelling at speeds between about 800 and 950 km/h (500 and 600 mph). Their objective is economical operation, not speed.

THE JET FAMILY

Practically all large planes now use jet engines for propulsion. A jet engine burns kerosene fuel in a combustion chamber. The hot gases produced shoot backwards out of the rear nozzle of the engine, and propel the engine forwards by reaction. (This is rather like a blown-up balloon shoots forwards when the air escapes backwards out of the neck). The jet engine is one kind of gas turbine. It has a turbine in the exhausting gas stream which spins a compressor that forces air into the combustion chamber.

There are three main kinds of jet engines. High-speed military planes use turbojets, which generally have one or two sets of turbines and compressors. For greater economy most airliners use turbofans. They are jet engines that have a huge fan at the front, which draws air not only into the engine but also around it (see picture top right). This produces a slower, broader jet stream that propels planes more efficiently.

The third main jet engine is the turboprop. This has an extra turbine in the jet exhaust which is used to spin a propeller. And this provides most of the propulsion. Turboprops are efficient but are only suitable for

Above: Heading into the setting Sun, a plane swoops down towards the runway. The approach lights help the pilot line up his craft for an accurate landing.

Inset left: A radio antenna like this is positioned at the end of the runway. It sends up a directional beam that planes lock onto when making an instrument landing.

relatively low-speed operation.

AIR-TRAFFIC CONTROL

There are so many airliners flying now that the airways are very closely watched by teams of air-traffic controllers at centres along the routes. They monitor the progress of each airliner by radar and radio communications. The pilots themselves navigate by means of radio beacons located on the ground beneath the airways.

The worst congestion in the air

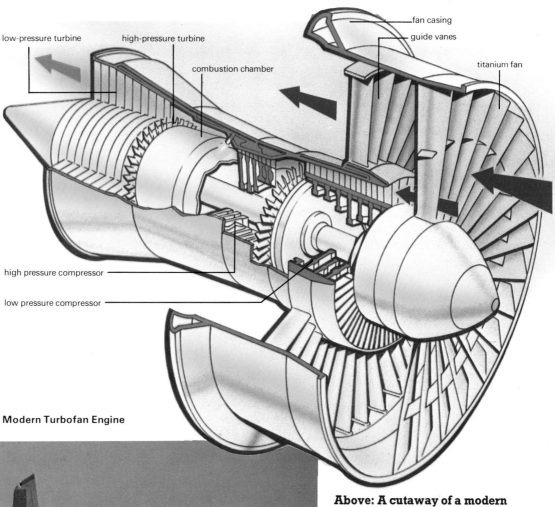

low-pressure turbine   high-pressure turbine   fan casing   guide vanes   titanium fan

combustion chamber

high pressure compressor

low pressure compressor

Modern Turbofan Engine

Above: Up in the control tower, a flight controller checks the location of aircraft on the airport runways with the ground radar.

Above: A cutaway of a modern turbofan engine, the type used on most airliners. A huge fan draws air into and around the engine.

Left: Airborne radars can monitor air-traffic movements in areas where there are no ground stations. This radar plane is the United States Air Force AWACS (airborne warning and control system) aircraft.

their path, it reflects the waves and returns them to the aerial as an echo. The echo then causes a spot to appear on a fluorescent screen. The word 'radar' stands for 'radio detection' and ranging.

The air-traffic controllers in the control tower have radars called the plan position indicator and the range height indicator. Together these radars tell the controllers the height, range and direction of every plane in the area. Pilots approach the runway with the help of the Instrument Landing Systems (ILS).

occurs in the vicinity of airports. New York's Kennedy Airport or London's Heathrow has to cope with as many as 1000 aircraft movements—take-offs and landings —every day. Often airliners have to 'stack', or circle at different heights over a nearby beacon until it is their turn to land.

RADAR AND ILS

The ground controllers use radar to guide the airline pilots down to the runway. Radar works by sending out pulses of high-frequency radio waves, or microwaves from a rotating aerial. If something is in

VTOL CRAFT

The letters VTOL stand for 'vertical take-off and landing'. There are three main kinds of aircraft that have this capability. They overcome the great drawback of ordinary planes—that they need a runway to take off and land. The runways at international airports average between about 2400 and 3000 metres (8000 and 10,000 ft) long.

The three kinds of VTOL aircraft are helicopters, or rotary-wing craft; fixed-wing craft with rotatable engine nozzles; and airships.

By far the most important are the helicopters, which have rotating flail-like blades on top of the fuselage. They were not the first rotary-wing craft, however. Juan de la Cierva built his rotary-wing autogyro in 1923. Igor Sikorsky did not demonstrate the first helicopter until 1939.

There are only two successful fixed-wing VTOL craft, both of them military. This is the British Aerospace Harrier, which first flew in 1960. Russia has a similar plane, Forger, first spotted in 1976.

The airship was the first successful powered aircraft, which pioneered long-distance aviation from the turn of this century. Disastrous accidents in the 1930s, plus the rapid development of the aeroplane killed off the airship as a major form of transportation. But there are signs that the airship is staging a comeback.

HELICOPTERS

In many respects the helicopter can be considered the perfect flying machine. Not only can it take off and land in its own length, it can also fly in any direction and hover with ease. Its only drawback compared with ordinary planes is that it is slow and very noisy. Most helicopters are now powered by gas-turbine, or turboshaft engines.

The most important part of a helicopter is its rotor—the blades that rotate on top of the body. These blades provide both the vertical lift and the forward propulsion. They form a rotary wing, and they do indeed have the same aerofoil shape as a plane's wing. So when they rotate, they develop lift, which supports the helicopter in the air.

For purely vertical flight, the

Top left: A Bell 214ST helicopter hauling a load seemingly bigger than itself. A 20-seater craft, it is powered by twin gas turbines and has a cruising speed of some 250 km/h (150 mph)

Left: A Sea King naval helicopter on the deck of the light aircraft carrier HMS *Invincible*. It is equipped for anti-submarine warfare.

pitch, or angle at which the rotor blades hit the air is the same for each blade. To go higher the helicopter pilot increases the pitch of the blades, which increases their lift. For horizontal flight the pitch of the blades is changed as they rotate. For forward motion, for example, the blades are given maximum pitch when moving downwind. In this way they sweep the air backwards and thereby propel the helicopter forwards.

Most helicopters, including the ones pictured on these pages, have a single main rotor. But notice that they also have a small rotor at the tail, which faces sideways. This is necessary to stop the body of the helicopter rotating when the blades rotate. The number of rotor blades can vary from two to eight.

Some helicopters have twin rotors, each rotating in different directions. This cancels out any tendency of the body to turn, and so no tail rotor is necessary. The rotors may be mounted one above the other on the fuselage, as in the Russian helicopter code-named Hormone, or separately, as in Boeing's successful Chinook.

A few helicopters, such as the Russian Hook, have short wings projecting from the fuselage, making them a hybrid craft, often called a compound helicopter. NASA's Ames-Moffett research centre has built experimental craft that can be modified to fly as a pure helicopter, a fixed-wing aircraft or a hybrid craft with wings as well as a rotor.

THE HARRIER

The Harrier achieves vertical take-off and landing by means of four swivelling nozzles, which direct the exhaust from its jet engines downwards. After the plane has climbed into the air the nozzles gradually swivel until they are pointing backwards. Then the jet exhaust can escape backwards and propel the plane in the usual way.

While the plane is moving vertically, it is kept level and stable

in the air by a reaction control system. This uses high-pressure air jets from the engine compressor.

AIRSHIPS

An airship consists of a large bag, or envelope, fitted with a gas that is lighter than air. Beneath the

Above: The Sikorsky SH-60B Seahawk, in service with the US Navy. It carries advanced surveillance and radar equipment, and is armed with two torpedoes.
Below: This British designed airship, like all modern ones, is filled with non-flammable helium gas.

Fact file . . .

Thirty-five people died when the 247-metre (810-ft) long airship *Hindenburg* exploded in New Jersey in 1937.

The Russian helicopter Mi-12, code-named Homer, is the world's largest, measuring 67 metres (220 ft) over its twin rotors and capable of lifting 40 tonnes.

envelope is a small passenger cabin, or gondola, which also carries the propellers that propel the craft.

The reason why the early airships were so dangerous was that they contained flammable hydrogen. Modern airships, therefore, are filled with helium which, though heavier than hydrogen, is non-flammable.

The large airships of yesteryear such as the Zeppelin *Hindenburg* and the *R101*, had a rigid skeleton beneath the envelope. Modern airships like the Goodyear *Europa* and the Skyship 500 do not. They are non-rigid 'blimps'.

ROCKETS & MISSILES

It is recorded that in the year AD 1232 the Chinese used 'arrows of fire' in their war against the Mongols. The 'arrows' are thought to have been rockets, not too different from the ones we see at fireworks displays. Rockets have been used on and off in warfare ever since. Now they are the most powerful weapons in the armoury of nations, because they can carry nuclear warheads over very great distances.

The first longish-range rocket missile was the German V2, developed as Hitler's second 'revenge weapon' during World War 2. After the war German rocket experts, plus captured V2s, were taken to the United States and Russia. They formed the nucleus of teams that by the late 1950s had developed rockets that could launch satellites into orbit, and ten years later send men to the Moon and probes to the planets.

ROCKET PROPULSION

The main problem about sending anything into space is gravity, or the Earth's pull. To overcome this pull, we must give an object a speed of at least 28,000 km/h (17,500 mph) or about 10 times the speed of a rifle bullet!

There is only one kind of engine that is powerful enough to achieve this speed—the rocket. Also, the rocket is the only kind of engine that can possibly work in space. This is because it not only carries fuel, but also carries oxygen to burn its fuel. Other engines, such as jets and petrol engines, have to take in air from the atmosphere. Therefore they won't work in airless space.

Rockets work by burning fuel and an oxidizer (oxygen-provider) inside a chamber. The hot gases produced then escape backwards out of the rocket nozzle. The force of them shooting out backwards sets up a force acting forwards that propels the rocket. This is the principle of reaction.

An American Delta rocket thunders from the launch pad at Cape Canaveral in Florida, carrying a Galaxy communications satellite.

Right: A Pershing 2 short-range military missile, which is fired from a mobile launcher. It can carry a nuclear warhead.

ROCKET PROPELLANTS

The fuel and oxidizer of a rocket are called its propellants. The humble firework rocket has gunpowder as propellant, which contains fuel and oxidizer mixed together. It is called a solid propellant. The space shuttle also uses solid propellant in its booster rockets. It is a mixture of aluminium powder and oxidizer.

Mostly, however, space rockets use liquid propellants, which are much more powerful. The Saturn V Moon rocket burned kerosene (paraffin) as fuel and liquid oxygen as oxidizer as it took off. The space shuttle uses liquid hydrogen as fuel and liquid oxygen again as oxidizer.

In a liquid-propellant rocket the propellants are stored in separate tanks and pumped into the combustion chamber, where they mix and burn. To achieve the great thrust needed to get into space, they burn propellants at a phenomenal rate.

LAUNCH VEHICLES

Even though rockets are tremendously powerful, a single rocket cannot make it into orbit. It

Above: A Tomahawk cruise missile leaps into the air after its launch underwater from a submarine. Later its rocket booster will be jettisoned and its turbofan engine will take over.

Right: A cutaway of the best-known of all space rockets, the Saturn V. This 111-metre (365-ft) high rocket launched Apollo spacecraft to the Moon.

hasn't got a high enough power-to-weight ratio. To overcome this problem, several rockets are joined together usually end to end for space launchings. The bottom one fires first and gives the ones above it a boost, and then it falls away. The second rocket fires and gives a further boost to the ones above it, and then falls away in turn.

In this way no deadweight is carried, enabling the rocket at the top of the stack to achieve the required speed to get into orbit. This kind of launching rocket is called a step rocket, or multistage rocket, and each individual rocket in the stack is called a stage.

Three-stage rockets are common. The American Delta rocket has three main stages. A cluster of solid rockets around its first stage give it extra thrust at lift-off.

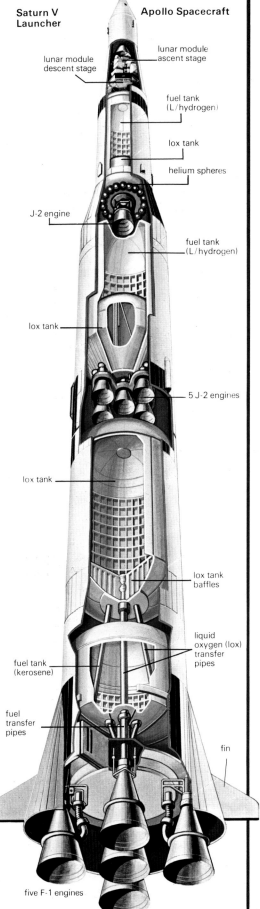

Saturn V Launcher — Apollo Spacecraft

lunar module descent stage
lunar module ascent stage
fuel tank (L/hydrogen)
lox tank
helium spheres
J-2 engine
fuel tank (L/hydrogen)
lox tank
5 J-2 engines
lox tank
lox tank baffles
liquid oxygen (lox) transfer pipes
fuel tank (kerosene)
fuel transfer pipes
fin
five F-1 engines

SPACE SHUTTLE

Until November 1982 all satellites had been launched into orbit by expendable rockets—rockets that could be used only once. But in that month an extraordinary new re-usable launch vehicle went into commercial operation. It was the space shuttle. It launched not one, but two communications satellites.

Since that time the shuttle has not only revolutionized satellite launchings, but also the whole of in-orbit space activity. Crewed by as many as eight astronauts, it has taken part in spectacular satellite recovery and repair missions. It has carried into orbit fully equipped space laboratories called Spacelab. In the 1990s it will ferry up parts from which a permanent space station will be constructed.

BLASTING INTO ORBIT

The space shuttle consists of three main components. The most important one is the orbiter, which carries the astronaut crew.

Four operational orbiters were built—*Columbia*, *Challenger*, *Discovery* and *Atlantis*. Tragically *Challenger* exploded just after lift-off in January 1986, killing a crew of seven, including the first 'ordinary citizen' to attempt a space flight, teacher Christa McAuliffe.

The orbiter looks much like a stubby airliner. It has a fuselage, swept-back delta wings and a tail. It measures some 37 metres (122 ft) long and has a wing-span of 24 metres (78 ft).

The orbiter takes off from a launch pad like a rocket, and it has three rocket engines in its tail. On the launch pad it is mounted on a huge external tank. This holds the liquid

With all engines blazing, the space shuttle blasts off the launch pad. Riding the shuttle stack this time is *Columbia*, the first operational orbiter. Within 10 minutes it will be in orbit.

Inset left: Orbiter *Columbia* glides in to land after another successful mission. It took off like a rocket, but now lands like a plane.

hydrogen and liquid oxygen propellants for its engines. Attached to the sides of the tank are two rocket boosters fuelled by solid propellants.

On lift-off the orbiter's main engines and the boosters all fire together, blasting the shuttle into the heavens with a thrust of some 3 million kg (6.5 million pounds). After about two minutes the boosters run out of fuel and fall away. They parachute into the sea, from where they are recovered to be used again.

The orbiter's engines continue firing for a further six minutes, driving it to the edge of space. Then their fuel tank runs dry, and falls away. But it isn't recovered. Finally, the orbiter fires two small engines of the so-called orbital manoeuvring system (OMS), which speed it up to some 28,000 km/h (17,500 mph). At this speed it goes into orbit.

ORBITAL ACTIVITIES

Up in orbit the astronaut crew open the doors that run along the upper fuselage of the orbiter. This reveals a huge payload (cargo) bay, measuring some 18 metres (60 ft) long and 4.6 metres (15 ft) across. It is nearly large enough to hold a railway carriage! But usually it just holds satellites and experimental equipment.

The astronauts carry out most of their work in orbit on the flight deck, the upper of two decks in the orbiter fuselage. The two pilot-astronauts are in charge of flying the orbiter into and out of space and manoeuvring it in orbit. The other astronauts don't fly the craft, but are responsible for launching the satellites and the scientific work. Some, called mission specialists, are professional astronauts like the pilots. Others, however, called payload specialists, are scientists who usually fly into space only once to look after particular experiments.

The mission astronauts work mainly at the rear of the flight deck. There are located the controls

and instruments for launching the satellites and operating the equipment in the payload bay. Most satellites are sprung or rolled out of the payload bay into orbit. But some are literally placed into orbit by a kind of 'space crane', known as the remote manipulator arm. The astronauts use the arm not only to lift satellites from the bay into space, but also to capture satellites already in space.

The main crew quarters are on the mid-deck of the orbiter. On this deck there is a galley, or kitchen unit, for preparing the meals. There is a sleep area, where astronauts sleep inside sleeping bags strapped to the walls. There is a lavatory which is flushed with air, not water. There is also an airlock on the mid-deck. The astronauts pass through this when they have to leave their craft to go spacewalking in order to maintain or carry out routine checks on the outside of the spacecraft and complete necessary equipment checks and adjustments.

RETURNING TO EARTH

When the time comes for the astronauts to return to Earth, they close the payload-bay doors and then manoeuvre the orbiter until it is travelling tail first. They fire the OMS engines once more as a brake; the orbiter slows down and drops from orbit.

It re-enters the atmosphere travelling at 25 times the speed of sound. Air friction heats up the outside of the orbiter to temperatures as high as 1500°C. To withstand such heat the orbiter is covered with tens of thousands of heat-resistant tiles made of silica (see page 71). This protects the mainly aluminium airframe and the astronauts inside.

Soon the orbiter is travelling much more slowly and is flying with its wings. A series of rolls and turns further reduces its speed to a few hundred kilometres an hour, and it swoops steeply down to land, like a plane, on an ordinary runway.

SATELLITES & PROBES

On average the Earth gains an artificial moon, or satellite, every few days. They are launched into space by a powerful rocket or the space shuttle. We can place a satellite into orbit about 300 km (200 miles) high by giving it a speed of at least 28,000 km/h (17,500 mph). At this speed, known as orbital velocity, it will continue circling round the Earth without falling down. The satellite is in space, but still bound to the Earth by gravity.

If we give an object a speed of no less than 40,000 km/h (25,000 mph), however, it will be able to escape from Earth completely. This speed is Earth's escape velocity. Spacecraft must be given speeds greater than this to reach the planets. We call such spacecraft 'probes'.

MESSAGES THROUGH SPACE

Most of the satellites that are launched each year are communications satellites. They pass on, or relay, communications signals over long distances between one location and another, often between the continents. They handle all kinds of signals, such as telephone conversations, radio messages, television signals, Telex calls, facsimile and computer data (see page 16).

The signals are beamed up to the satellite from one telecommunications network via a huge dish antenna. The satellite

Right: The X-ray satellite *Einstein* produced this image of the star Alpha Centauri, showing it is bright at X-ray wavelengths as well as in visible light.

receives the signals, strengthens them and then beams them back down to another dish antenna, which passes them onto another telecommunications network. The latest satellites of the International Telecommunications Satellite Organization (Intelsat), Intelsat VAs, can handle 15,000 simultaneous telephone conversations and two TV channels transmitting colour programmes.

Most communications satellites these days are lofted into a high orbit, some 35,900 km (22,300 miles) above the equator. At this height and location, they circle around the Earth in exactly 24 hours. Because they thus keep pace with the Earth, they appear 'fixed' in the sky. Such an orbit is called a geostationary, or 24-hour orbit.

WEATHER WATCH

Our weather forecasting, like our communications, has been revolutionized by satellite technology. Cloud-cover pictures and data provided by weather satellites enable forecasters to keep track of weather systems everywhere on Earth.

Many weather satellites, such as NOAA, circle over the North and South Poles. They view the weather situation over the whole of the Earth

Fact file . . .

Since 1982 more than 350 lives have been saved by a satellite search and rescue (sarsat) system.

When the Voyager 2 probe reported back from Uranus in January 1986, the radio signals took 2¾ hours to travel the intervening 3000 million km (1864 million miles).

A look inside a European communications satellite. The solar panels unfold in orbit and face the Sun. They produce the electricity to power the electronics and communications systems.

Key
1 Solar panels, partly unfolded
2 Communications antennas allowing up to 7,200

telephone circuits simultaneously
3 Antenna platform
4 Thermal blankets
5 Communications

every day as it spins beneath them. Some weather satellites, however, operate from geostationary orbit. They keep an eye on the weather over one particular part of the Earth. The European Meteosat weather satellite is located in geostationary orbit over West Africa. It shows the weather conditions over the Atlantic Ocean, Africa, Europe and the Middle East.

EARTH WATCH

A third important kind of satellite takes pictures of the Earth's surface, but not in ordinary light. Its electronic 'eyes' see in light of different 'invisible' wavelengths such as infrared. At such wavelengths they can pick out details in the landscape that are invisible in ordinary light.

The pictures, or images they take can show where there is disease among crops; where there may be valuable mineral deposits beneath the surface; where there is flooding or pollution. Such images are also invaluable to map-makers.

The best-known of the Earth-watching satellites is the American Landsat. The latest of the series, Landsat 5, scans the Earth from a height of about 700 km (435 miles). Some 4 metres (14 ft) long, it has an Earth weight of about 2 tonnes.

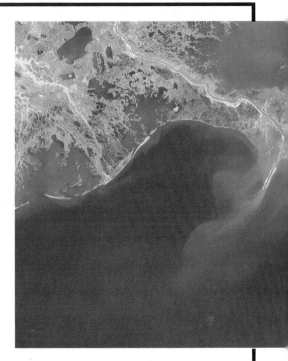

Above: Landsat provided this false-colour image of the Mississippi Delta region in the southern United States. The pale blue shows the muddy sediment being washed into the sea by the river. Vegetation shows up red.

ORBITING OBSERVATORIES

A fourth class of satellites looks out into the universe rather than down to Earth. They are astronomical observatories, whose telescopes and other instruments gather the radiation the stars give out. Practically all the satellite observatories 'look' at the universe with the help of invisible wavelengths, such as X-ray, gamma-ray, ultraviolet and infrared. We cannot study these radiations on Earth because they are blocked by the atmosphere.

These orbiting observatories have sent back remarkable information about the universe to scientists on Earth. They have discovered regions where there could be the infamous black holes, which swallow all nearby matter as well as light. They have seen where new stars are being born. They have spotted what appear to be solar systems around other stars.

modules for telephone and television transmissions at 11 and
14 GHz.
6 Service module
7 Thruster tanks
8 Steerable solar panel mounting

CHAPTER 3

FUEL AND POWER

In our power-hungry world we still rely on the fossil fuels coal, oil and natural gas to supply the bulk of our energy needs. We also harness on a large scale the energy in flowing water and in the nuclear fission of uranium atoms. In our search for alternative power sources we exploit the energy that is blowing in the wind, driving the tides, and streaming through space from the Sun. There is a possibility that nuclear fusion, too, will contribute to our needs.

Ablaze with light in the middle of the North Sea are two of the production platforms in the Forties oil field. Oil is now the world's most important fuel, but supplies could run out early next century.

FOSSIL FUELS

Some three hundred million years ago much of the Earth was covered by swamps and warm shallow seas. In the swamps grew huge plants, much like present-day ferns and horsetails but as tall as trees. When the plants died, their remains fell into the swampy ground and began to decay. Then rivers washed mud over them. More plants died, fell, started to decay and were buried.

After millions of years, heat and pressure inside the Earth's crust caused the layers of mud and plant remains to harden. The mud turned into rock, the plant remains into the black 'mineral' we call coal. Coal has been one of the world's most useful fuels for centuries. Because it is the remains of something that was once living, we call it a fossil fuel.

ROCK OIL

The warm shallow seas of that same period of the Earth's history also teemed with life. They contained an abundance of tiny plants and animals not unlike the plankton found today. When these organisms died, they fell to the bottom of the sea and decayed into a slimy ooze.

The ooze became covered with mud and sandy sediments that eventually changed into rock. The ooze turned into the greenish-black liquid we call petroleum, or crude oil. It became trapped in the rock layers, where we find it today. Petroleum is another fossil fuel, more important now than coal.

Gas was formed at the same time as the liquid petroleum. This also became trapped inside rock formations, and we tap it today as natural gas. This is our third valuable fossil fuel.

COAL GRADES

Coal is a good fuel because it contains a high proportion of carbon. Carbon burns in the air to form carbon dioxide, giving out heat.

The lowest-grade coal, called brown coal or lignite, contains up to about 65 per cent carbon. The highest-grade coal, anthracite, can contain more than 90 per cent carbon. In between come the bituminous coals, the type most widely used for domestic and industrial purposes. In some parts of the world people use peat as fuel. It is partly decomposed vegetable matter that is well on the way to becoming coal.

HYDROCARBONS

Petroleum is not a single chemical

Right: A giant rotary bucket excavator working at an opencast coal mine in Russia. The wheel digs into and scoops up the coal as it rotates. The buckets tip the coal onto a conveyor belt, which carries it to the rear.

Below: A Condeep oil production platform is towed out into the North Sea oil fields. Constructed in concrete, it will weigh more than 350,000 tonnes when completed.

Above: Crude oil only becomes useful when it is processed in an oil refinery like this. Here it is separated into its components.

substance, like water is, but is a mixture of hundreds of different substances with one thing in common. They are made up of hydrogen and carbon only.

They are organic chemicals, whose molecules contain chains of carbon atoms. This is not unexpected, because they are the remains of once living things, and all living things, ourselves included, are made up of such carbon-chain chemicals.

Natural gas also consists of hydrocarbons, but much simpler ones. The main one is methane, whose molecules contain just a single carbon atom attached to four hydrogen atoms. We represent it by the chemical formula CH_4. Other hydrocarbon gases include ethane (C_2H_6), propane (C_3H_8) and butane (C_4H_{10}).

Propane and butane are interesting in that they readily turn into liquids under pressure. They are then bottled and sold as bottled gas, which serves as a valuable portable fuel for ballooning, among other things. Bottled gas is known as LPG, liquefied petroleum gas.

COAL GAS

People were using gas in their homes and factories long before natural gas was discovered. It was made by destructively distilling coal—heating it without air. The gases produced included methane, hydrogen and carbon monoxide.

When the supplies of natural gas and petroleum run out, large-scale production of coal gas will almost certainly be resumed. The gas-making process also produces two valuable by-products, coke and coal tar. Coke is an excellent fuel in its own right, while coal tar is a rich source of chemicals for industry.

Fact file . . .

The biggest oil platform, Statfjord B, in the North Sea oilfields, weighs more than 815,000 tonnes, and is the heaviest object ever to have been moved on Earth.

About 2–3 million million barrels (1 barrel = 160 litres, 35 gallons) still remain in the Earth's crust.

HYDROELECTRICITY

Most of the electricity produced in the world is generated using energy obtained by burning fossil fuels. But about a quarter is generated using the energy of flowing water. It is known as hydroelectricity.

The largest power stations in the world are hydroelectric. The Grand Coulee power station in Washington State, USA, has an output of some 10,000 megawatts. This is enough to satisfy the power needs of several million homes.

Most hydroelectric power schemes involve the building of a dam across a river to form an artificial lake, or reservoir. The water level behind the dam rises, and this 'head' of water provides the power. The water is led from the reservoir through tunnels (called penstocks) into water turbines located near the foot of the dam. They spin the turbines, and also the electricity generators that are coupled to the turbines. The energy in the water flowing down from the high level of the reservoir is converted into electricity.

WATER TURBINES

The water turbine is a modern version of the waterwheel. This was the first mechanical power source mankind discovered, about 2000 years ago. It was in widespread use until the 1800s, when it was replaced by the steam engine.

The modern turbine that makes use of a similar principle to the waterwheel is called the Pelton wheel. It is a wheel with buckets arranged around its edge. Jets of water are directed against the buckets and force the wheel round. Some wheels are mounted so that they rotate in a vertical plane, like a waterwheel; others rotate horizontally.

The water turbines used in most hydroelectric power schemes, however, are quite different. They generally resemble a ship's propeller. Water spins the turbine blades as it flows through. The most common turbine type is called the Francis. Water enters this turbine radially, or from the sides, and leaves it axially, or along the axis. In another widely used type, the Kaplan, the water flows into and out of the turbine along the axis.

The Pelton wheel is most suited to a high-head site so that the water leaves the jets and hits the turbine at high speed. The Francis turbine is suitable for both high and low heads. The Kaplan is particularly useful where there is a low head but a high volume.

A tidal-power plant is an unusual kind of hydroelectric scheme, which makes use of the twice-daily ebb and flow of the tide to generate power. A barrage holds back the ebbing or flowing tide until there is a reasonable 'head' of water. This is then allowed one way or the other through the turbines. The first major tidal-power plant was built across the estuary of the River Rance in Brittany, France, in 1966.

PUMPED STORAGE

In some of the latest hydroelectric schemes the same water is made to flow through the turbines time and time again.

The idea is that during the day the hydroelectric plant operates in the usual way. Electricity is produced when water flows down from a high reservoir, through the turbines and produces electricity. Then at night, when demand for electricity is low, water is pumped back up into the reservoir, ready for use again the following day. This principle is known as pumped storage. The pumping may be done by separate pumps, or by turning the turbines themselves into pumps.

One of the world's most advanced pumped-storage schemes operates in North Wales at Dinorwig, Gwynedd. It uses a head of 530 metres (1740 ft) and has an output of 1880 megawatts.

A look at the inner workings of a pumped-storage hydroelectric scheme. Power is produced when water flows down through the inlet pipe (13) into the turbine (15), which spins the generator (5). When pumping, the pump (30) draws in water through the inlet pipe (32) and pumps it up through the discharge pipe (26).

Key

1	Transformer	18	Relief valve
2	Valve controls	19	Guide vanes
3	Gantry crane	20	Turbine governor
4	Valve pits	21	Oil coolers
5	No. 1 generator	22	Oil pumps
6	Access hatch	23	Coolant system
7	No. 2 generator	24	Governor oil pump
8	Bearing	25	Water outlet
9	Cooling fan	26	Discharge pipe
10	heat exchanger	27	Pump coupling
11	Rotor windings	28	Discharge valve
12	Stator windings	29	Valve servo
13	Turbine inlet	30	Storage pump
14	Inlet valve	31	Impeller
15	Reaction turbine	32	Pump inlet
16	Guide vane servo	33	Pump inlet gate
17	Relief valve servo	34	Oil filter

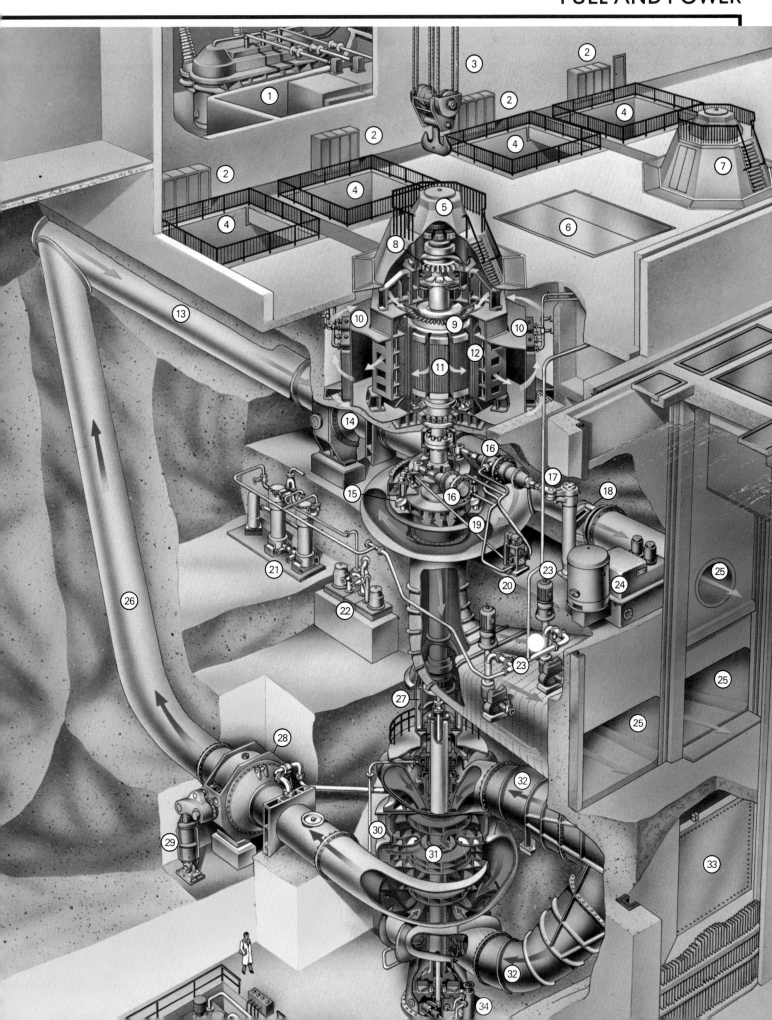

NUCLEAR POWER

What do you think is our best fuel—wood, coal, oil, natural gas? No, it is a metal called uranium. In theory we could get from 1 kg (2.2 lb) of uranium, the same amount of energy that we get by burning 3000 tonnes of coal!

However, uranium is not a fuel in the usual sense. We don't burn it to produce heat. Instead we split up its atoms, or rather the centre of the atoms, the nucleus. When we split a uranium nucleus, tremendous energy is given out. We call it nuclear energy. We call the splitting process fission.

CHAIN REACTION

Fission occurs when a certain mass of uranium is brought together. Then a chain reaction takes place, with the fission of one atom triggering off the fission of others in rapid succession. If the chain reaction is not controlled, so much energy will be released so quickly that a devastating explosion will take place. This is what happens in

the dreaded atomic bomb.

Fortunately we have found a way of controlling the chain reaction so that the energy can be released slowly. And we can harness that energy for good, rather than evil. We control the chain reaction and extract the nuclear energy by means of a nuclear reactor.

NUCLEAR REACTORS

More than 200 power stations throughout the world use nuclear reactors to produce heat for generating electricity. They use the heat to boil water into steam, which then drives the steam turbines that spin the electricity generators.

There are several kinds of reactors, but they all work on similar lines. The uranium 'fuel' is held in a core. Control rods are pushed into and pulled out of the core to control the rate at which the chain reaction takes place. They thus control the heat output from the reactor.

The heat is removed from the

Above: The power locked inside the nucleus of atoms is enormous. When it is released suddenly, as in a hydrogen bomb, it creates the most catastrophic explosion, producing temperatures of millions of degrees.

Right: Fuel rods are stored under water after they have been removed from a reactor. This is done to reduce their radioactivity. The radiation the rods give out causes this fascinating blue glow.

core by a coolant. The hot coolant circulates to a heat exchanger, where it gives up its heat to water. This boils into steam for feeding to the generating turbines.

One of the commonest kinds of power-station reactors uses water under pressure as the coolant. Such pressurized-water reactors are also used in nuclear submarines. An advanced kind of reactor uses liquid sodium metal as a coolant. It is called a breeder reactor because it produces more fuel than it uses. The drawback is that this fuel is

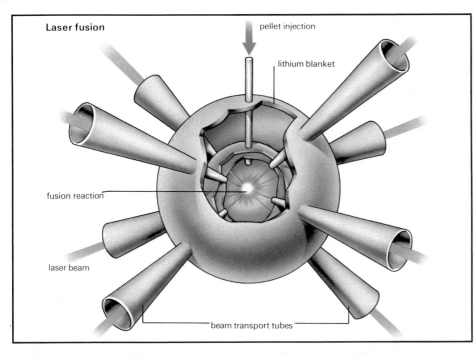

Laser fusion

pellet injection

lithium blanket

fusion reaction

laser beam

beam transport tubes

Left: Some scientists are trying to bring about nuclear fusion by means of powerful lasers. They fire a battery of lasers from all directions at a tiny heavy hydrogen target. The heat from the fusion reaction is removed by a blanket of lithium.

plutonium, which is one of the deadliest substances known.

RADIATION RISKS

Plutonium is deadly, not only because it is poisonous in itself but because it gives out penetrating radiation--it is highly radioactive and will be for tens of thousands of years. Uranium and the products of fission in the reactor are also highly radioactive.

The radiation these substances give out damages the body tissues. It can cause sickness, burns and, in large doses, a very unpleasant death. Even in small doses it can alter the genes in the body cells and in this way affect future generations. In a nuclear power plant, therefore, the reactor is heavily shielded.

Below: An outline of a pressurized water nuclear reactor (PWR). The heat from controlled nuclear fission in the fuel elements heats up water into steam. The steam drives a turbo-generator to produce electricity. The nuclear reaction is controlled by pushing the control rods in (reduce the reaction rate) and out (increase the reaction rate).

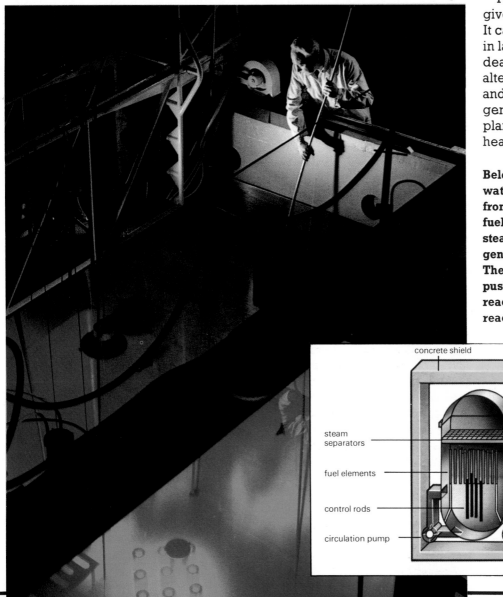

concrete shield

generating turbine

steam

steam separators

fuel elements

control rods

circulation pump

condenser

water

feed pump

ALTERNATIVE ENERGY

When we switch on the electric light, fill up the car with petrol or light the gas fire, we are using up precious resources. The coal, oil and natural gas we so heavily use as fuels took hundreds of millions of years to form.

Oil and natural gas supplies will start to dwindle before the end of this century. And coal will not last for too much longer if that becomes our major fuel once more.

So what will we do then? We could use more nuclear fuel, but that would lead to a greater radiation risk. And in any case, supplies of uranium 'fuel' are also limited. For future energy needs we must look elsewhere.

SUN POWER

The most obvious source of endless power is the Sun, which pours onto our planet many thousands of times more energy than we will ever need. And it will continue to shine at the rate it does now for several thousand million years to come. The problem is that solar energy is thinly distributed. On average only about one kilowatt of solar energy (the equivalent of a one-bar electric fire) falls on each square metre of the Earth's surface.

Nevertheless we are finding ways of capturing this heat and putting it to work. We can heat the water in our homes by solar power using flat-plate collectors (illustrated opposite). But a different system is needed if we are to harness solar energy on a large scale.

Near Albuquerque, New Mexico, Sandia Laboratories have constructed a 'power tower' scheme. Banks of mirrors, or heliostats, concentrate sunlight onto a receiver atop a 60-metre (200-ft) high tower. When such a scheme goes commercial, the heat will be concentrated on a boiler that will produce steam to drive turbogenerators to make electricity.

Next century huge solar power satellites could be built high above the Earth to harness the Sun's energy. They would consist of solar reflectors or banks of solar cells. The energy they collect would be beamed down to the Earth in the form of microwaves and converted into electricity. To produce a reasonable power input the satellite would have to be several kilometres long, and require maybe 100,000 tonnes of constructional materials.

Man has used the energy blowing in the wind and carried by flowing water for thousands of years, typically for milling grain and pumping.

Some people in remote areas already use small wind turbines to generate electricity. And some countries are experimenting with very large wind turbines to produce power commercially. NASA's Lewis Research Center, based in Ohio, has developed huge propeller-type machines that are feeding power into the electricity grid in various parts of the country. One of the most powerful is the machine at Medicine Bow, Wyoming, which has a 78-metre (256-ft) long rotor blade and a power output of 4 megawatts.

The energy of flowing water is already being harnessed on a large scale in hydroelectric schemes (see page 56). And the ceaseless surge of the ocean's tides is also being tapped, most successfully at the Rance estuary in Brittany, France. Other likely sites for tidal-power schemes are the Severn estuary in England and the Bay of Fundy in North America. Other schemes have been suggested to tap the energy of ocean waves, using hinged floats, called ducks, and oscillating water columns.

OTEC

The huge floating structure shown right illustrates an idea for extracting heat from the surface waters of tropical oceans. It is known as OTEC (ocean thermal energy conversion).

In the OTEC plant an easy-to-vaporize liquid, such as ammonia, would be evaporated by the heat of the surface waters, at a temperature of perhaps 30°C. The vapour would expand through turbines, which would spin generators and produce electricity. The vapour would then be condensed back into liquid by cold water piped up from the ocean deeps, where the temperature might be only 5°C. The generating plant would be located near the surface. The pipe for carrying up the water from the depths would need to be 500 metres (1600 ft) long.

Some schemes seek to extract the heat locked in underground rocks in volcanically active regions of the world. Such geothermal power is already being tapped in Iceland, California, France and New Zealand. In some areas underground sources of hot water are piped to heat buildings. In others pipes are sunk to pockets of steam and fed to turbogenerators.

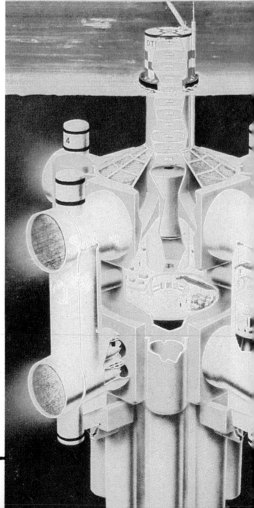

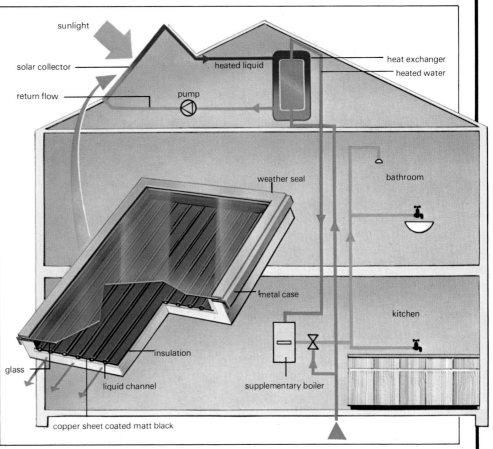

sunlight
solar collector
return flow
pump
heated liquid
heat exchanger
heated water
weather seal
bathroom
metal case
kitchen
insulation
glass
liquid channel
supplementary boiler
copper sheet coated matt black

Above: One method of using solar heating in houses. A liquid is pumped through pipes in a solar collector panel which traps heat rather like a greenhouse does. The heated liquid then circulates to a heat exchanger, where it heats water.

Below: In some parts of the world volcanic activity is being harnessed to produce power. Water is heated by the underground rocks and turned to steam, which is piped to turbogenerators to produce electricity. This is geothermal power.

Above: A traditionally designed windmill for harnessing the power blowing in the wind. The windmill can drive a generator to produce electricity or work a pump for pumping water for drinking and irrigation.

Left: This complicated piece of hardware could soon be seen in tropical oceans. It would generate power using the heat of the ocean's waters.

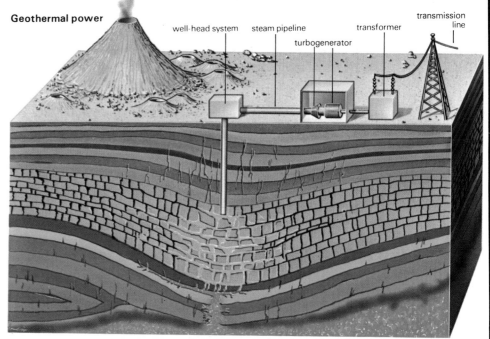

Geothermal power

well-head system · steam pipeline · turbogenerator · transformer · transmission line

POWER SUPPLY

Electricity is by far the most convenient form of energy we have. It is on tap at the flick of a switch to power the cooker, lights, TV set, vacuum cleaner and sewing machines, as well as lathes, milk floats and locomotives. Before it reaches our homes and factories the electricity has travelled maybe hundreds of kilometres from the power station in which it was produced, or generated.

In the power station the electricity is produced by machines called turbogenerators. They consist of a turbine coupled with an electricity generator. In most power stations the turbine is spun by high-pressure steam. In hydroelectric power stations the turbine is spun by fast-flowing water (see page 56).

In conventional steam power stations the steam is produced in water-tube boilers. Water turns into steam when it is run through pipes in the flue of a furnace in which coal or oil is burned. In nuclear power stations the steam is produced when water is heated by a nuclear reactor (see page 58).

Above: The turbine hall in a conventional power station. The steam turbines are housed within the casings on the left of the picture.

Opposite: The central control room of a nuclear power station near Leningrad, which supplies the city with 2 million kilowatts of electricity.

Left: The large turbine wheels of a steam turbine dwarf the engineer working on them. The largest wheels are used for the low-pressure stages of the turbine.

STEAM TURBINES

In a steam power station steam is fed to the turbines at temperatures as high as 600°C and at pressures of over 300 atmospheres (300 times ordinary atmospheric pressure). The turbine consists of a long shaft that rotates inside a casing. The rotor shaft carries a series of multi-bladed wheels of different sizes. Each set of rotor blades is called a stage.

The steam spins the rotor shaft as it expands through the turbine blades. Each set of blades has a larger diameter than the one before it. In this way the maximum energy can be extracted from the steam as it expands and its pressure drops. Usually the sets of blades are housed inside separate cylinders at high, intermediate and low pressure. The blades in the low-pressure cylinders are several metres across. To improve the flow of steam through the turbine, the

Fact file . . .

A large power station requires up to 250 million litres (55 million gallons) of cooling water every hour.

On 9/10 November 1965 30 million people in the north-eastern United States and Canada suffered the biggest power failure in history, lasting up to 13 hours.

low-pressure turbine exhausts to a condenser, where the steam changes back into water.

ELECTRICITY TRANSMISSION

The turbines spin the electricity generators at about 3500 revolutions per minute. A single turbogenerator will produce 500 megawatts of electricity or more. And a power station will have perhaps four such units. Typically the voltage ('pressure') of the electricity produced is 25,000 volts AC. AC stands for 'alternating current', current that flows first one way then the other, 50 or 60 times a second.

The electricity is carried from the power station to the consumers by overhead transmission lines, slung from high steel towers, or pylons.

It would not be practical to transmit electricity at 25,000 volts over long distances. Too much power would be lost. For efficiency, the electricity must be transmitted at voltages as high as 400,000 volts or more. Fortunately, there is an easy way of boosting, or stepping-up the generated voltage, and that is by transformers.

The transmission lines carry electricity to substations, which organize distribution to consumers. The high transmission voltage has to be gradually reduced, or stepped-down again by transformers to levels that the customers use. Factories use voltages up to about 30,000 volts, while homes only require 230 volts.

THE GRID

To even out the supply of electricity over a region or even a whole country, power stations are usually linked into a network, or grid system. They, as it were, pool their resources so that they can cope when unusual demands occur in particular areas.

Britain has the world's largest grid system. Some 140 power stations can supply up to 55,000 megawatts at any time. Even greater flexibility is provided by submarine links with the French grid system, that have a total capacity of some 2000 megawatts.

CHAPTER 4

RAW MATERIAL

The discovery and use of metals put mankind on the road to civilization, and today they form the foundation, or perhaps we should say the skeleton, of our technological age. Wood, clay and natural fibres play their part in the modern world as they did in pre-metal, Stone Age times. But they are being outstripped in importance by materials not found in nature, particularly plastics and synthetic fibres.

Electronic circuits exploit to the full the properties of the materials they use. The various components are mounted on an insulating plastic board. A thin film of copper is printed on the baseboard to connect the components. The components are fixed in place in the printed circuit by the quick-setting alloy solder. The most intriguing materials — wafers of silicon — are hidden inside the black plastic blocks. They each hold thousands of miniaturized circuits.

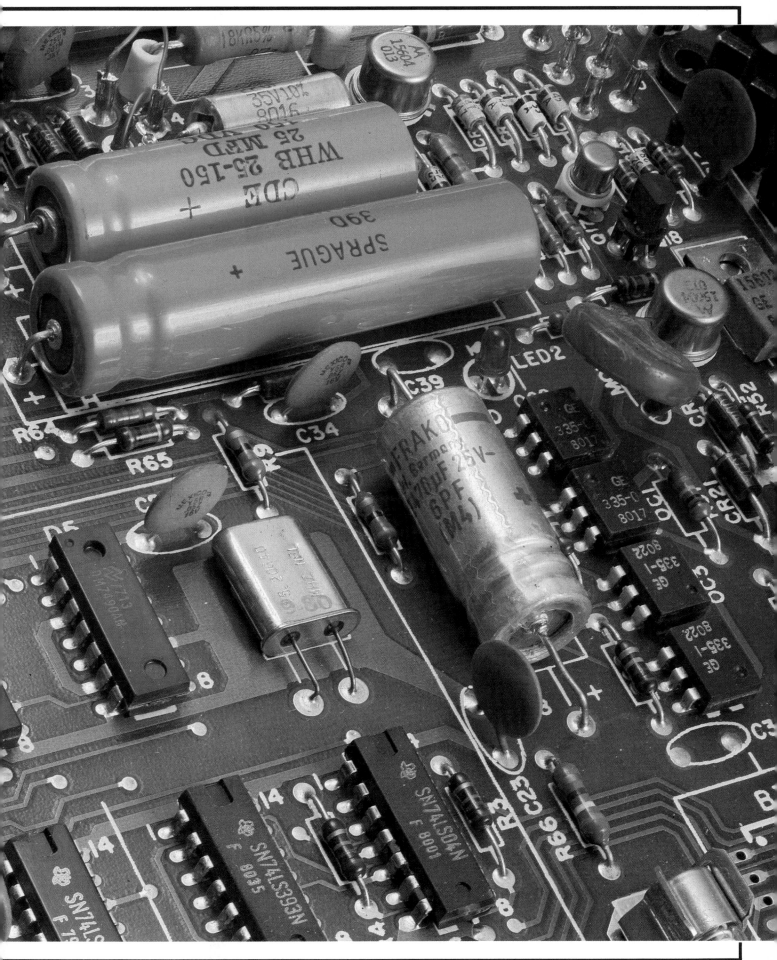

Civilization as we know it today could not exist without metals. Without metals we could not make the machines that produce practically all the goods we use. We would still be living in a Stone Age, where stone, wood, clay and bones would be our main materials.

The Age of Metals began perhaps as long as 10,000 years ago, when prehistoric people found lumps of natural metal, such as copper, gold and iron from meteorites. But it was so scarce that it was generally fashioned into jewellery and ornaments rather than tools and weapons.

Then people discovered how to extract metals from minerals in the ground. They made copper first (about 5000 BC) and then bronze (about 3500 BC), an alloy, or mixture of copper and tin. The world entered a Bronze Age. In turn this gave way to an Iron Age (from about 1500 BC). Iron dominated civilization until the middle of last century, when Henry Bessemer (in 1856) discovered a cheap method of making the iron alloy steel.

Fact file . . .

Gold is the most ductile (easily stretched) of metals: 1 kg can be drawn out into nearly 2500 km of wire (1 lb can be drawn out into nearly 700 miles).

A nickel-iron alloy called invar scarcely expands or contracts at all when the temperature changes.

THE AGE OF STEEL

We are still living in a Steel Age, even though we have discovered many other metals unknown to the ancients. Steel is made by purifying pig iron from the blast furnace. It is mainly iron with traces of manganese and carbon.

It is the carbon that gives steel its toughness and strength. The ordinary steel used to make car bodies, for example, has up to about 0.25 per cent of carbon and is known as mild steel. As the percentage of carbon goes up, the steel gets harder and tougher. High-carbon steels (up to 1.5 per cent carbon) are widely used for making cutting tools, drills and saws.

ALUMINIUM AND COPPER

The dominance of iron and steel in our world can be seen from its production figures compared with other metals. Some 500 million tonnes of steel are produced annually worldwide, compared with only about 11 million tonnes of aluminium and some 6 million tonnes of copper. The other metals, of which there are over 60, are produced in even smaller

Above: Ships' propellers are made from alloys such as brass or bronze. These metals are easy to cast into shape and resist the corrosion of the salty sea water.

Below: An offshore oil production platform being towed out to sea. It is made from ordinary steel protected from corrosion by bars of magnesium or zinc.

quantities.

Aluminium has become one of our most important metals because of its most outstanding property—lightness. It is only about one-third as heavy as steel but can be made into alloys that are just as strong. Aluminium also has the advantage that it does not rust away, or corrode like ordinary iron and steel do. One major use for aluminium is for making aircraft and spacecraft, where lightness is essential. In the home its uses range from pots and pans (it is a good conductor of heat) and kitchen foil to greenhouses.

Copper, our most ancient metal, has a multitude of uses in the electrical industry because it is a superb conductor of electricity. Most electrical wiring is copper. Copper tubing is now widely used for home plumbing. The metal is also an ingredient in many alloys,

including brass, bronze and cupronickel. All have widespread uses in and out of the home.

All the different metals we use have different properties—some good, some not so good. Iron, for example, is strong but rusts. Copper, tin and zinc do not corrode, but are soft. Seldom does a particular metal have all the properties we would wish. But we can often improve matters by mixing two or more metals together.

By mixing copper and tin we get the alloy bronze, and by mixing copper and zinc we get brass. Both bronze and brass have the desirable property of their parents—corrosion resistance, but they are also hard. By alloying we have improved the properties of both metals.

In a similar way we add chromium and nickel to iron to make a steel that doesn't rust. We call it stainless

Below: This Japanese temple has a roof made of stainless steel, chemically treated so that it is black. The blue colour in the picture is the reflection of the sky. Notice how different the temple looks to the other buildings.

Right: The intake fan of the massive Pratt and Whitney PW2037 turbofan engine, which powers many Boeing 757 airliners. Aircraft engines have to be constructed of special alloys which remain strong at high temperatures.

steel. Nickel, in fact, is one of the most versatile of alloying metals. With copper it forms cupronickel, the alloy used for our 'silver' coins. With chromium it forms a series of nichrome alloys, notable for their heat resistance and widely used in jet and rocket engines. Chromium is included in steel alloys designed for making tools that must run at high speeds. Also included is tungsten, the most heat-resistant of all metals. These tool steels keep a sharp cutting edge even when they run red-hot!

WOOD

FARMING THE FOREST

Trees are among the most important of the world's natural resources, for they provide us with wood. We use the wood in solid form as timber to build our homes. We break it down into pulp for making into paper, artificial fibres and chemicals.

In prehistoric times vast forests covered much of the land areas of the world. When people became farmers, they gradually began to clear the forests for their crops. Today the greatest forest area stretches in a broad band across the northern parts of North America, Europe and Asia. Dense tropical forests are also found straddling the equator in Africa, Asia and South America.

In many countries forests are 'farmed'. Young trees are planted as the older ones are cut down. But

Right: Heavy machines are now widely used in the forests to fell and extract the timber. Aerial cable systems are also often used for extraction.

Below: The lengthy process of paper-making. Wood chips are processed chemically or are ground into pulp. Pulp sheets are then mixed with water and the mixture is beaten to fray the fibres. After adding such materials as china clay, size and colouring matter, the pulp mixture flows onto the Fourdrinier paper-making machine. There the water is removed and a layer of pulp fibres is squeezed together and dried to form paper sheet.

elsewhere the forests are being 'mined', with no thought for the future. This is happening particularly in the great rain forests of tropical regions, where the delicate balance of nature is being upset and many wildlife species are facing extinction.

As so often in the modern world, the great problem is over-consumption. It is reckoned that a forest the size of Sweden has to be cut down each year just to supply the world's paper.

In the cool northern forest regions thrive the conifers (cone-bearing) trees, such as the pines and firs. Most of them have needle-like leaves and are evergreen. These trees are known as softwoods, and in general their wood is relatively soft. The softwoods are our most important source of timber for both construction and pulpmaking.

In the temperate regions of the world grow the hardwood trees, whose wood is generally harder. These trees, which include ash, oak, beech and birch, have broad leaves which they shed each year in autumn. The hardwoods that grow in the tropical forests also have

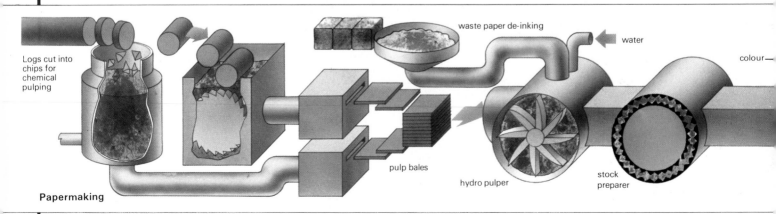

Logs cut into chips for chemical pulping

waste paper de-inking

water

colour

pulp bales

hydro pulper

stock preparer

Papermaking

broad leaves. But they shed leaves a few at a time and are never bare like those which come from the world's more temperate regions.

DOWN IN THE FOREST

In most European and American forests the trees are felled and removed with mechanical equipment. The fellers use noisy but deadly efficient chain saws that slice through the trunk of a tree in minutes. They consist of an endless chain carrying saw teeth, which is driven by a tiny petrol engine.

SAWMILLS AND PULPMILLS

From the forest the timber is taken either to the sawmills or the pulpmills. At the sawmills various kinds of power-driven saws slice up the logs into boards and other familiar forms of timber. Three main kinds of saws are used.

The band saw consists of an endless steel band edged with saw teeth, which travels at high speed in a vertical plane. The frame saw has a number of parallel sawblades

Left: Logs are often transported from the forest to the pulpmills by water, as here on a lake in Denmark. The water helps protect the logs from fire.

Below: Logs need to be shredded into small chips before they can be used to make chemical pulp. Here a mountain of chips awaits pulping.

mounted on a frame, which moves rapidly up and down. The circular saw has saw teeth around its edge and cuts as it rotates.

At the pulpmill one of two methods may be used to reduce wood to pulp. In the mechanical process, small logs are shredded by a revolving grindstone. In the chemical process the logs are cut into tiny chips, which are then 'cooked' with chemicals. This releases the fine wood fibres, which are largely cellulose. The pulp from either process is dried into sheets for despatch.

At the papermill the pulp is once again mixed with water to form a porridgy mass. This is then beaten in a stock preparer to fray the fibres and make them more flexible. Various additions are made to it, such as size and dyes, before it flows onto the Fourdrinier papermaking machine.

As the liquid pulp is carried along by a fast-moving belt, the water drains away, assisted by suction. It turns into a damp web of matted fibres. Next the damp web passes through a series of heavy rollers which squeeze out more water and press the fibres tightly together.

The damp sheet then passes round a series of drying cylinders, heated by steam in the so-called 'dry end' of the machine. Finally a stand of heavy polished calendar rollers impart a smooth shiny finish to the paper. The whole papermaking machine can be up to 90 metres (300 ft) long, and the paper may come off it at speeds up to 100 km (60 miles) an hour.

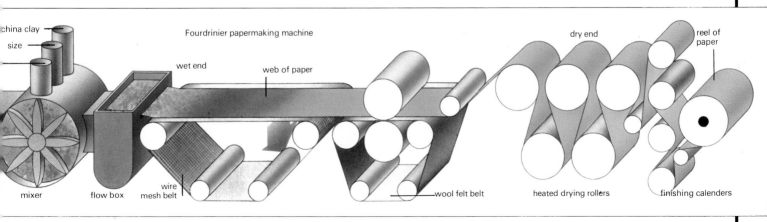

china clay
size
Fourdrinier papermaking machine
dry end
reel of paper
wet end
web of paper
mixer
flow box
wire mesh belt
wool felt belt
heated drying rollers
finishing calenders

CERAMICS

One of the first materials early peoples used was clay they dug out of the ground. They found that when clay was moist, it could be fashioned into bowls, pots and jugs. They then put the clayware into the hot embers of a fire, and baked it. So began the craft of pottery, practised as widely now as then.

Pottery is one kind of ceramics—materials that are made from clay or a similar earthy material and baked in a fire or kiln (oven). We use a great many other ceramic products today, including bricks, tiles, cement, glass and synthetic gems.

POTTERY AND PORCELAIN

The ordinary pottery used for plates and cups and saucers is made of earthenware. It is baked, or 'fired' at about 1000°C, and is relatively soft and porous. By itself it will not hold liquids, so it is given a surface glaze, or glassy coating to make it watertight and also more attractive.

The finest pottery, porcelain, is quite different. It is brilliant white in colour, not dull like earthenware. And it is glassy not only on the surface but all the way through. It is also translucent, and gives out a clear ring when you strike it (softly!). Porcelain is made using a pure white clay called kaolin or china clay. It is fired at temperatures up to 1400°C.

It is often called china because it was the Chinese who first made porcelain over 1000 years ago.

BRICKS AND CEMENT

The first bricks were made many thousands of years ago from mud mixed with grass or straw, which helped bind the mud together. Mud bricks are still used for house-building even today in some hot countries such as Egypt and Mexico. Such adobe houses are surprisingly long-lasting.

Modern bricks are fashioned from clay. A suitable clay mix is kneaded and then extruded as a continuous ribbon of rectangular cross-section. A set of wires slices the ribbon into brick-size blocks. Some bricks are alternatively made by pressing the clay in moulds. After being dried in hot air, the raw clay bricks are fired in a kiln.

In ordinary building work bricks are bonded together with mortar. This is basically a mix of fine sand and cement, with some lime or

Below: Glass bottles are made automatically by high-speed machines. Streams of molten glass are cut into gobs, which are placed in hollow moulds and then blown into shape.

Fact file . . .

The compound tantalum carbide is the most refractory substance known, melting at 3990°C.

The glass used to make optical fibres is so pure that a block 20 km (12.5 miles) thick would be as transparent as ordinary window glass.

Below: Stages in the production of float glass, a perfectly flat glass with a brilliant finish. It is made by floating a ribbon of molten glass on a bath of molten tin.

Float glass process

- 46% sand
- 26% cullet (broken glass)
- 13% soda
- 11% dolomite
- 3% lime
- 1% saltcake

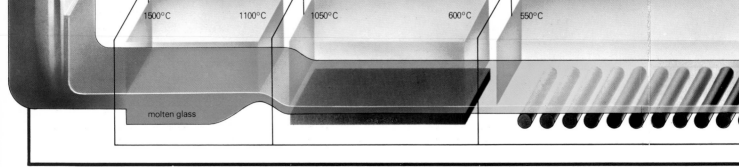

melting furnace — 1500°C — 1100°C — float bath — 1050°C — 600°C — 550°C — molten glass

other material added. Cement is a fine grey powder made by roasting crushed limestone, clay, ore and other materials in a huge rotating kiln. When mixed with sand, gravel and water, cement turns into hard-as-rock concrete, one of our foremost constructional materials.

REFRACTORIES

Special bricks are required in industry to line the insides of industrial furnaces. They must be able to withstand very high temperatures without melting or breaking up. Such bricks are made from materials with a high content of heat-resistant, or refractory materials, such as silica, dolomite

Right: Fixing heat-resistant tiles to the underside of a space shuttle orbiter. Made from pure silica fibres, each tile is unique, being identified by a computer number.

annealing lehr

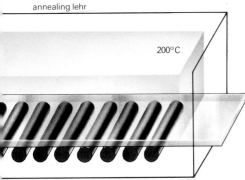

200°C

or alumina.

Silica is one of the finest refractories. It is used, for example, to make the tiles that act as a heat shield for the American space shuttle. Alumina too has excellent heat resistance. It is used for the insulating body of car spark plugs.

GLASS

Silica is also the main constituent of glass, a substance that really has remarkable properties. It is very cheap, transparent, can be easily shaped, and is unaffected by all common chemicals save one—hydrofluoric acid.

Included with silica in the recipe for ordinary window glass are soda ash and limestone. The glass is called soda-lime glass. The three materials, plus a little scrap glass (called cullet), are heated in a

furnace to a temperature of about 1500°C. At this temperature the raw materials melt, or fuse together to form a red-hot liquid. When the liquid cools, glass forms.

Different kinds of glass are made by varying the glass-making recipe. Coloured glass can be made by including certain metal oxides. A tough heatproof glass can be obtained by including some boric oxide.

Including lead oxide in the glassmaking recipe produces a dense glass that has a very attractive sparkle, which can be brought out by expert cutting. This results in the so-called cut glass or lead crystal glass. In the nuclear power industry glass with a very high lead content is used for the windows of rooms where radioactive materials are kept. The lead stops radiation escaping.

PLASTICS

Over the past 40 years the use of plastics has grown to such an extent that it would be difficult now to imagine life without them. Plastic products abound in the home—bowls, squeezy bottles, bags, electrical plugs, telephones, curtain rods, and ping-pong balls.

The ping-pong ball is included in the list because it has important historical connections. It is made of celluloid, and celluloid was the first successful plastic made. It was first introduced by New York printer John Hyatt in 1869 as a substitute for ivory.

THE SYNTHETICS

Another milestone in plastics history came in 1909. In that year a Belgian-born chemist, Leo Baekeland, synthesized a resinous substance while experimenting with formaldehyde and the coal-tar chemical phenol. He found he could mould the resin by heating. He had discovered the first synthetic plastic. Whereas celluloid was made from a natural material, wood cellulose, Baekeland's plastic was made from chemicals. We still use his plastic, called Bakelite, even today.

But it was in the 1930s and early 1940s that the true foundations were laid for our 'Plastics Age'. In quick succession chemists manufactured perspex, polyethylene, nylon, polystyrene, polyesters, PVC (polyvinyl chloride) and epoxy resins. All these are now produced on a vast scale, accounting for the bulk of the 50 million tonnes or more of plastics that are used annually in the world.

POLYMERS

One thing common to all plastics is that their molecules are very long. They are made up of long chains of atoms with a 'backbone' of carbon atoms, as the picture (top right) shows.

In the manufacture of synthetic

Right:
A polyethylene (polythene) molecule is made up of long chains of carbon atoms linked together. To each is attached two hydrogen atoms.

Below: A pole vaulter bends his plastic pole at a seemingly impossible angle as he leaps upwards.

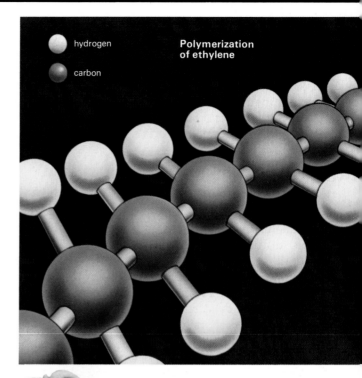

hydrogen

carbon

Polymerization of ethylene

plastics the long-chain molecules are built up by linking together many small molecules. Polyethylene, for example, is made by linking together thousands of molecules of ethylene (ethene), which has the chemical formula C_2H_4.

Ethylene is known as the monomer ('one part'); polyethylene, the polymer ('many parts'); and the process, polymerization. The names of most of the other plastics mentioned so far also indicate how they are formed. For example, polystyrene is made by polymerizing the chemical styrene.

Most of the chemicals used for making synthetic plastics, such as ethylene and styrene, come from petroleum. They are obtained by processing the crude oil in oil refineries. The starting point for cellulose plastics, such as celluloid and cellulose acetate, is woodpulp or cotton linters (the fibres around cottonseeds). They make use of the naturally occurring long-chain molecules that make up cellulose.

THERMOPLASTICS AND THERMOSETS

There is quite a difference between the plastics used for washing-up bowls and the better quality plates and cups. The bowls are often made of polyethylene, the tableware of melamine-formaldehyde. If you accidentally leave the bowl on an electric hot plate, it will melt. But if you leave the plate on it, it will either be unaffected or will burn or crack. It will not melt.

Polyethylene is a kind of material called a thermoplastic or thermosoftening plastic. It will melt again when it is reheated. Most of our plastics are like this. Melamine-formaldehyde on the other hand is known as a thermoset, or thermosetting plastic. It sets rigid when it is first shaped and remains rigid when reheated.

SHAPING PLASTICS

One general property common to all plastic materials is that they can readily be shaped by heating and, usually, moulding. This makes plastic products easy and cheap to mass-produce. Thermoplastics are easiest to shape because they stay molten all the while they are hot. Thermosets, however, start to become rigid as soon as they are heated, and so they require a different moulding technique.

Thermoplastics are commonly shaped by injection moulding or blow moulding. In the injection method, molten plastic is injected under pressure into a mould, and takes the shape of the mould when it cools. In blow moulding, air is blown inside a 'gob' of molten plastic inside a cool mould.

Thermosets are most commonly shaped by compression moulding. Moulding resin powder is placed in the bottom half of a heated mould. The top half of the mould is then forced down onto it, forcing the melting powder into shape as it sets.

Extrusion is another common shaping method for thermoplastics. The plastic is melted and then forced by a rotating screw through a die of the required shape, emerging at the other end rather like toothpaste being squeezed from a tube.

Below: The body shell of this experimental car is made from tough coloured plastic, mounted on a rigid steel skeleton. It has a working life of at least 20 years.

FIBRES

People first discovered how useful fibres were at least 9000 years ago, when they began domesticating sheep. They found they could spin the wool fibres into continuous yarn, which they could then weave into fabric. For the first time they could make comfortable clothes instead of wearing uncomfortable animal skins.

We still make our clothes today by spinning and weaving fibres. Spinning is the process in which short fibres are gathered together into a loose 'rope', which is then drawn out and twisted. This produces a continuous strong thread, or yarn. Weaving is the process of interlacing lengths of yarn under and over one another to make cloth.

Spinning occupies an important place in the history of technology, because it was the first process to become highly mechanized. This resulted from a series of inventions in England in the 1760s and 1770s, including the spinning jenny and the spinning mule. Richard Arkwright capitalized on these inventions by installing machines in a mill and employing workers to operate them. This founded the factory system of manufacture and spearheaded the Industrial Revolution.

NATURAL FIBRES

Wool, the original fibre, is still used on a vast scale. The finest wool comes from the Merino breed of sheep. An adult Merino ram can yield up a fleece weighing up to 13 kg (28 pounds). Other animals that provide wool include the Angora and Cashmere goats. Cashmere is exceptionally soft. The Angora goat's hair is better known as mohair.

But the finest animal fibre of all is silk. This is a fine lustrous thread produced by the silkworm, which is actually the larva of a moth. Unlike the other natural fibres, silk is produced as a long thread, or continuous filament.

The world's most widely used fibre, though, is cotton. Cotton fibres are found around the cotton seed in the seed pod, or boll. Another useful vegetable fibre is found in the stalks of the flax plant. This is the fibre used to make linen.

RAYONS

Many of the fibres used these days to make fabrics are not to be found in nature. They are produced by chemical processes in factories. One of the first to be made, and still the most widely used, is rayon. It was called artificial silk when it was first introduced because it has a silky lustre and feel.

The kind of rayon produced today, viscose, is made by treating

Below: Different forms of carbon fibre. It is used to reinforce plastics, producing an exceptionally strong and lightweight material.

Right: A telephone cable made, not of copper wires, but of optical fibres. Each fibre can carry hundreds of telephone calls at the same time.

woodpulp or cotton linters (short fibres) with chemicals. The cellulose in these materials dissolves. Then the solution is pumped through a spinneret, a cap with many tiny holes, into an acid bath. The streams of solution react with the acid, and turn into continuous threads of cellulose.

Other fibres are made by dissolving cellulose in acids and then solvents, and pumping them through a spinneret into the air. They are called acetate and triacetate fibres.

SYNETHETIC FIBRES

Another very large group of fibres are the synthetics. Nylon was the

Right: These lightweight hawsers are made from Kevlar fibre, yet they are as strong as those made from steel.

Below: Carbon-fibre reinforced plastics are used in the Boeing 767, fast becoming the most popular airliner in its class.

Above: This high-speed knitting machine is using nylon yarn to make tights. Nylon stockings ushered in the synthetic-fibre fashion era in the 1940s.

first one made, by the American chemist W.H. Carothers in 1935. He made it from chemicals extracted from coal tar. These days nylon and most of the other synthetic fibres are made, like plastics, from petroleum chemicals. Indeed they are plastics that can be drawn out into fine fibres. The most important ones besides nylon are the acrylics and the polyesters.

Nylon fibres are made by pumping molten nylon through a spinneret. Polyester and acrylic fibres are made by pumping solutions through a spinneret. Compared with natural fibres, the synthetics are stronger, do not rot and are not attacked by moths.

They are easy to wash and 'drip-dry' quickly. They also resist creasing.

SPECIAL FIBRES

Several other interesting kinds of fibres are produced, but they are not used for making textiles. Glass can be made into fibres readily by melting it and forcing it through fine holes. One of the main uses of glass fibres is for reinforcing, or strengthening plastic compositions. The material we generally call fibreglass, from which we can mould car bodies and boat hulls, is properly termed glass-reinforced plastic (GRP). A different kind of pure glass fibre is ushering in a new era in telecommunications.

One of the most remarkable artificial fibres is carbon fibre. It also finds its greatest use in reinforcing plastics. Carbon-fibre composites are very rigid and have four times the strength, weight for weight, as high-tensile steel. They are being increasingly used in aircraft construction.

CHAPTER 5

INDUSTRY

Two-and-a-half centuries ago people's working life began to change fundamentally. Instead of making goods with their hands, they began making them in factories with machines. There was an Industrial Revolution. Today, machines dominate all aspects of industry, from mining and refining to manufacturing and farming. Increasingly they are coming under automatic, computer control, making for greater efficiency and freeing the human workforce from much industrial drudgery.

Industry has come more and more under computer control in recent years. The use of computer-controlled machines and processes allows more economical production and often releases the human workforce from boring and repetitive tasks.

MINING

People began mining in prehistoric times, and one of the first things they mined was flint. They needed the flint to make their tools and weapons. They discovered that flint flakes readily when struck, yielding a sharp cutting edge. Later, the discovery of smelting processes to produce metals led to an increasing demand for ores for smelting.

Today vast amounts of ores are extracted from the ground to provide the raw materials of our modern world. The United States and Russia between them extract some 300 million tonnes of iron ore each year. As well as ores, mines supply us with coal, native metals such as gold and platinum, diamonds, salt and other minerals. The other major products 'mined', though we don't use the term, include petroleum and natural gas.

SURFACE MINING

The easiest kind of mining is that which takes place on or near the surface. It is called opencast mining, or sometimes open-pit or strip mining. When stone or gravel is extracted at the surface, this is called quarrying not mining. Coal, iron ore, copper ores and bauxite (aluminium ore) are often taken from opencast mines. They are removed by power shovels or excavators. Massive dragline excavators (see opposite) may be needed to remove any soil, or overburden, covering the deposit.

Some gold, diamonds and heavy ores like cassiterite (tin ore) can often be found in gravels in stream beds, lakes and on the sea shore. They have been concentrated there by the action of running water, into so-called placer deposits. Mining consists of different methods of sorting out the heavy minerals from the loose gravels.

GOING UNDERGROUND

Only part of our mineral wealth lies conveniently close to the surface. Much is buried deep underground. In South Africa miners have penetrated nearly 4 km (2½ miles) deep following the gold veins at the Western Deep Levels Mine at Carletonville. But this is an exceptional depth for mining, economical only because of the richness of the veins. In Britain, for example, the deepest mines (coal) in current use are a little over 1100 metres (3600 ft) deep.

In a typical underground mine, vertical shafts are sunk through the rock strata holding the ore or coal. Then tunnels are dug horizontally to reach the deposits. Most ores are hard and must be shattered by explosives before they can be extracted. Much coal is extracted in a similar way, but much is also cut out by machine. This is possible because coal is relatively soft. Coalcutting machines called shearers and trepanners have rotating toothed cutter heads that slice along the coal seam layer by layer, working along a long coalface under the protection of a row of hydraulic props. They are

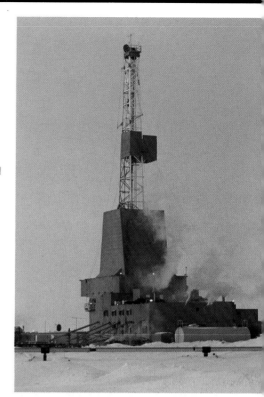

called 'walking props' because they advance progressively as the coal seam recedes.

DRILLING

Drilling for oil and gas is done from a tall drilling rig. The structure is needed to lift the drill pipes into and out of the hole being drilled. The hole is drilled by rotary action. Lengths of pipe are linked together, the bottom one carrying a drill bit. On the face of the bit are a number of toothed wheels, sometimes tipped with diamonds.

When the drill bit is rotated, the wheels turn and grind their way into the rocks. A liquid mud is pumped down through the hollow drill pipes. This lubricates and cools the bit and removes the cut rock. If and when gas or oil is struck, the borehole is capped by a set of valves to control the flow.

Drilling is now carried out increasingly at sea, following the discovery of many offshore oil deposits, such as in the North Sea. It is done from drill ships and special semisubmersible drill rigs, which operate in water down to a depth of 200 metres (650 ft).

Fact file . . .

The Bingham Canyon opencast copper mine in Utah is the world's largest excavation, measuring over 3 km (2 miles) across and more than 790 metres (2600 ft) deep.

Using modern coalcutting machines, miners can extract up to 1000 tonnes of coal underground in an hour.

Left: The search for minerals and mineral fuels takes geologists to the most remote corners of the Earth. Here in Arctic Alaska they are drilling for oil in temperatures way below freezing for most of the year.

Right: Deep underground, the teeth of a shearing machine bite into the coal seam. A chain conveyor carries away the cut coal.

Below: This walking dragline excavator scoops up 50 cubic metres (65 cubic yards) of top soil with one bite of its digging bucket. Its boom is 80 metres (265 ft) long.

EXTRACTING

SMELTING

However, the commonest way of extracting metals is by smelting, or heating their ores in a very hot furnace. This may need to be done in several stages before a reasonably pure product is obtained. The later purifying stages are usually termed refining.

The most important of all smelting processes is that used for iron ore, which is carried out in a blast furnace. In the smelting process, iron ore and coke are charged into the top of the blast furnace, together with limestone. The purpose of the limestone is to combine with the earthy impurities in the ore. Inside the furnace the coke burns fiercely as hot air is blasted in from hot-blast stoves. It reduces the ore to iron, which is molten at the 1500°C temperature inside the furnace.

The molten iron trickles downwards and collects at the bottom of the furnace. The limestone and impurities form a molten mixture called slag, which collects as a layer on top of the molten iron. Periodically the slag and iron are separately tapped. The molten iron, called pig iron, is then usually poured into a travelling ladle and transferred to other furnaces for refining.

STEELMAKING

The pig iron coming from the blast furnace still contains too many impurities to be useful as it is. But when it is refined it becomes steel, our most useful constructional material.

The most important method of making steel today is a development of a process developed by Henry Bessemer in 1856. In the Bessemer process steel was made cheaply for the first time by blowing air through molten pig iron. The modern equivalent is called the basic-oxygen process, which differs in that pure oxygen

Out of all the minerals we mine from the ground, the most important by far are the ores. These are compounds containing metals combined with other chemical elements, from which the metals can economically be extracted. Processing ores is the only way we can get most metals because they are too reactive to be found in metal form. The exceptions include platinum, gold, silver and copper. Of these, platinum and gold are the only two mined in metal form on a large scale.

Some metals are extracted from

Tall distillation towers dominate an oil refinery. In these towers crude oil is separated into its various 'fractions', to be used as fuels or chemical raw materials.

their ores by treatment with chemicals to form a solution. The solution may then be electrolysed, which means that electricity is passed through it. This results in the pure metal being deposited. Copper can be extracted in this way. Electrolysis can also be used to extract metal from an ore when it is molten, as with aluminium.

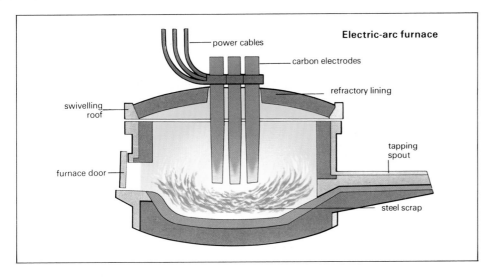

Electric-arc furnace

power cables

carbon electrodes

refractory lining

swivelling roof

tapping spout

furnace door

steel scrap

is blasted into the molten pig iron. Limestone and steel scrap are also charged into the cone-shaped basic-oxygen furnace. Impurities either burn out or combine with the limestone to form a slag. The refining process is very quick, taking less than 45 minutes to produce over 300 tonnes of steel.

The finest steel, however, is made in an electric furnace and from graded steel scrap only. It is essentially a remelting process. It takes place usually in an arc furnace. The heat to melt the scrap is provided by an electric arc stuck between the scrap itself and massive carbon electrodes overhead. The furnace is tilted for emptying.

Above: The finest steel is made in the electric-arc furnace from steel scrap. The heat is produced by a powerful electric arc, struck between carbon electrodes and the scrap itself. The scrap is charged into the furnace through the movable roof. The furnace is emptied by tilting.

petroleum separate out at different levels according to their boiling points. Gases come off at the top, petrol comes from the first tray (coldest), and heavy oils from the bottom tray (hottest).

Further refinery processes change the less desirable heavier oil 'fractions' into more petrol and useful chemicals. The most important of these processes is cracking, which splits apart large molecules into small ones. The reverse process of polymerization (see page 73) is also carried out on refinery gases, again yielding petrol and more useful chemicals.

The cracking is carried out in a tall, narrow tower under very high pressure, and in the presence of chemical catalysts that speed up the reaction to an economic rate. In the future, a similar process may be used to enable coal to be converted into liquid fuel.

REFINING OIL

Petroleum, or crude oil, comes out of the ground as a thick, greenish black liquid, which, as it is, is not very useful. But it can readily be processed, or refined into a host of valuable products—fuels, lubricants, and chemical raw materials for making into such things as plastics, synthetic fibres, drugs, dyes, and insecticides.

The first process in an oil refinery is distillation. The oil is vaporized and then fed into a tall fractionating tower, which has trays at different levels maintained at different temperatures. In this tower the various substances (called hydrocarbons) in the mixture that is

Below: In a blast furnace, iron ore is heated fiercely with coke and limestone. The ore is reduced to molten iron and a molten slag that contains earthy impurities. The 'pig iron' produced needs further refining before it can be used.

Blast furnace

limestone
iron ore
sinter
coke

skip winding gear

top bell

lower bell

furnace gas to cleaning plant

gas outlet

refractory lining

hot blast stoves

hot air blast

melting zone

tuyère

skip bridge

bunkers

loading skip

slag notch

tap hole

MANUFACTURING

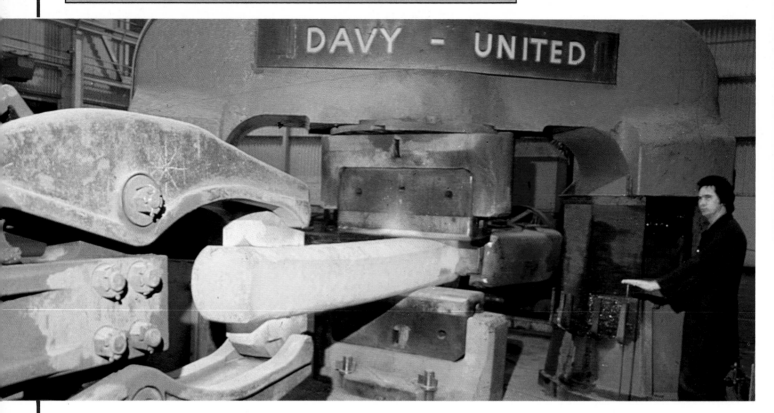

In general we can describe manufacturing as a process or series of processes that transforms raw materials, such as metals or plastics, into finished products. Often the products are made up of a number of different parts joined together. And a typical manufacturing operation involves the shaping of the parts, finishing them to the required standard of accuracy, and assembling them.

The word 'manufacturing' is not a particularly good one to describe the production of goods in the modern world. It literally means 'making by hand', and there are few goods indeed these days that are made by hand. Almost everything is made by machine. The human hand is involved merely in operating the machine. But often these days even this is unnecessary since many machines control themselves or are controlled by other machines, such as computers.

SHAPING PROCESSES

Metals dominate the manufacturing scene, so we shall concentrate here on methods of shaping and finishing metals. But many of them have parallels in methods used to shape other materials such as plastics, glass and wood.

Metal may be shaped in a variety of ways, when molten, red-hot but solid, and cold. It is shaped in the molten state by casting in moulds. A typical mould is made out of a sand/clay mixture. It is made by packing the sand around a model of the object to be cast. When the model is removed, a cavity of the required shape remains. Molten metal is then poured in and takes the shape of the cavity when it cools. In another form of casting hot metal is injected into water-cooled metal moulds (dies). This method, known as diecasting, is particularly suited for mass-production.

Hot but solid metal may be shaped in several ways. It can be rolled by a kind of mangle of heavy rollers, which can be shaped to produce things like girders and railway rails. The metal can also be hammered into shape by blows from the falling ram of a drop forge. This is the mechanical equivalent

Above: Metal shaping processes form an important part of manufacturing. Here a slab of titanium alloy is squeezed by a 2000-tonne press forge in preliminary shaping operations.

of the blacksmith, who has been practising forging for thousands of years. Alternatively, the metal can be pressed into shape by the gradual squeezing action of a giant hydraulic press.

In other methods metal parts can be shaped by forcing (extrusion) or pulling (drawing) the metal through a die. They can also be formed by fiercely heating metal powder (powder metallurgy) or with the aid of explosives (explosive forming).

FINISHING

The shaping methods outlined above seldom produce metal components that are ready for use. Much work usually remains to be done by machines that cut the metal accurately to size and shape, drill holes in it, plane it, grind it, or polish it. The machines that carry out these operations, which are

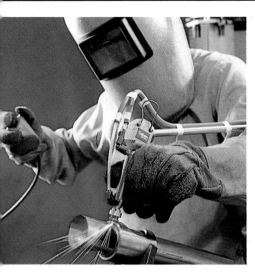

Above: For precision cutting and welding operations lasers are now often used.

Below: The factory floor in a modern car production plant. A decade ago it would have been swarming with people. Now automatic machines do much of the work.

Above: Most metal products require final shaping by machining. Computer-controlled lathes like this carry out the process automatically and accurately.

driven by powerful electric motors, are called machine tools.

Most important is the machine tool called the lathe, found in practically every factory and workshop. It is used to shape shafts and other objects of circular cross-section. The workpiece is rotated while cutting tools are moved into it at right-angles. The operation is called turning. Milling is another common machining process which involves the removal of metal by a rotating toothed wheel. In drilling, holes are bored in the workpiece with rotating drill bits. Grinding uses a moving belt coated with abrasive material to remove metal.

Not all metal objects need be shaped with high precision. Car bodies and oil production platforms, for example, can be shaped more crudely by welding. In welding, the edges of the two metals to be joined are placed in contact and heated fiercely until they soften and fuse together. More metal may be added from a filler rod. When the metal cools down, the joint is strong because the metal structure is continuous.

The two main methods of welding are arc welding and gas welding. Arc welding uses an electric arc; gas welding generally uses a mixture of oxygen and acetylene gas.

FOOD & FARMING

Prehistoric people led a precarious existence, forever at the mercy of the elements. For food they relied on gathering berries, fruits and wild grains, and hunting for meat. When Nature's food supply failed and hunting was unsuccessful, they starved. Not until about nine to ten thousand years ago did they begin actively growing plants themselves, and herding animals for their meat, wool and skins. They became farmers.

This was a key factor in the foundation of civilization. For not everyone had to spend their lives looking for food. There was time for the non-farmers to do other things, and this led to the development of technologies such as metallurgy and building, and the emergence of arts and crafts.

So farming can be regarded as the oldest industry, an industry that manufactures food. Like other industries over the years, it has benefited from mechanization. This began remarkably early, with the invention of the ox-drawn plough in about 3500 BC, more or less the same time the wheel was invented. But it was not until the 1700s and 1800s that the ancestors of our modern farm machines appeared—the seed drill (1701), mechanical reaper (1840), combine harvester (1854), and steam traction engine (1850s), which led to the modern tractor (1903).

FARM MACHINES

The tractor is the 'workhorse' on the farm these days which is used to pull carts and implements of many kinds—ploughs, harrows, seed drills, forage harvesters, mowers, crop sprayers, balers and so on. The standard tractor has two huge wheels at the rear to give it good grip and traction and two small ones at the front. It is powered by a diesel or petrol engine that drives the wheels via a clutch and gearbox. Some have four-wheel drive (see picture, page 31).

The tractor has two other interesting features. One is a power-take-off (PTO), which is a shaft from the gearbox that is used to drive cutter blades and the like of the implements it pulls. The other is a hydraulic lift mechanism, which is used to raise and lower the implements.

Among the other machines on the farm, the plough, the seed drill and the combine are particularly important. The plough has a number of curved blades that bite into and turn over the soil, so burying the weeds. The latest ploughs have as many as 12 blades, or 'bottoms', so they can turn 12 furrows at once. They can

comfortably plough over 4 hectares (10 acres) in a day. The seed drill, used for sowing cereals, holds the grain in a hopper and feeds it at a controlled rate through tubes into shallow furrows made by a disc or blade. A harrow pulled behind covers up the grain.

The combine harvester is so called because it combines the actions of reaping and threshing, that is, cutting the crop and beating the seeds from it. A rotating reel at the front of the machine directs the crop onto the cutter bar. The cut stalks are carried by elevator to a threshing drum where they are beaten. The grain and chaff drop down onto vibrating sieves, where the chaff is removed by an air blast.

The grain is carried by elevator to a storage tank. The chaff and straw are carried to the rear and discharged. Some combines cut a swathe as wide as 9 metres (30 ft) and can harvest over 4 hectares (10 acres) every hour!

FOOD PRESERVATION

These days we can not only enjoy the fruits of the farmer's labours in season, we can also enjoy them out of season. We can also enjoy foods from all over the world. This is thanks to modern methods of food preservation. To be successful preservation methods must prevent the food rotting, which can come about from the action of chemicals called enzymes in foods, and

Above: Machines have revolutionized farming as any other industry. They have been largely responsible for the great increase in productivity on farms in recent years. This modern rotary baler gathers hay into rolls.

through micro-organisms, such as moulds and bacteria, and through oxidation in the air.

There are three main preservation methods in common use—canning, freezing and drying. In canning, foods are packed into cans, which are then sealed and heated to high temperature in a pressure cooker. This treatment sterilizes the food, that is, kills any micro-organisms already present. Since the can is sealed, no organisms can

then exposed to a vacuum while being heated.

MANUFACTURING FOODS

As well as preserving farm products as they are, we also process them in various ways, for example; milk into butter and cheese, meat into sausages and paté, sugar beet into table sugar, and sunflower seeds into oil. Food chemists have also created products that are substitutes for traditional foodstuffs.

Frenchman Hippolyte Mège-Mouriés began it all in 1869 when he produced margarine as a substitute for butter from a mixture of animal fats and oils. Margarine today is made increasingly from vegetable oils, such as coconut, rape, and sunflower oils. They produce a lighter product that some consider healthier than butter.

A highly nutritious meat substitute is also widely available now, made from soya-bean protein. Soya-bean solids are ground into a kind of flour, mixed with a binding liquid and then spun into fibres. The fibres mat together to give a product with a meat-type texture.

subsequently enter. The 'tin' cans used are actually made of tinplate—sheet steel coated with tin.

Freezing preserves foods by slowing down the action of enzymes and preventing micro-organisms growing. If the freezing process is quick, the food texture is not much damaged by ice formation. Drying stops micro-organisms growing by removing the moisture they need. The modern method, called accelerated freeze drying, helps preserve the original texture and flavour of the food. The food is first frozen, and

Above: Mechanization comes to the dairy. The cows are milked during one turn of the rotary milking parlour.

Bottom left: This food-processing factory produces a perennial favourite, potato crisps.

Below: Here algae (inset) are growing in the waste water from a fish farm. They can be converted into a protein-rich food for the fish.

AUTOMATION

computer reacts to changing conditions and oversees all parts of the refinery at once.

The refinery provides one of the best examples of what is called automation, which means the use of machines that control themselves. Automation is now being introduced into many branches of industry, where it is bringing about what is often called the second Industrial Revolution. It is a logical development of a process that began during the first Industrial Revolution.

MECHANIZATION

The first Industrial Revolution was triggered off by mechanization, the introduction of machines on a large scale. This happened first in the textile industry in the 18th century with the invention of spinning and weaving machines. One of the inventors, Richard Arkwright, introduced another vital stage in the development of industry when in 1771 he installed a number of his spinning frames in a building, drove them by water power, and

If you visit an oil refinery, one thing immediately strikes you. Among block after block of tall, steel towers and pipes, there is scarcely anyone to be seen. It is like a ghost plant, yet things are obviously happening. Liquids gush through pipes, valves turn on and off, heaters cut in and cut out. So who or what keeps the refinery going?

The answer is a machine—a computer—in a central control room. This keeps the processes and machines within the plant working normally. It is linked to sensors, or measuring instruments in every part of the plant that feed information back to it about the conditions there. It holds in its memory a record of what the ideal conditions should be. If the actual conditions at any point vary from the ideal conditions, then the computer issues instructions to, say, a heater, valve or pump, to switch on or off so as to correct the error. The

Above: In many industries these days, as here in brewing, the manufacturing processes take place automatically. A computer is in charge of all the operations. The human operator checks on instrument readings displayed on monitor screens.

Below: Silicon chips (left), small enough to pass through the eye of a needle, are the 'brains' behind the latest automatic machines, such as robot welders (right). Robot welders are now widely used by car manufacturers throughout the world.

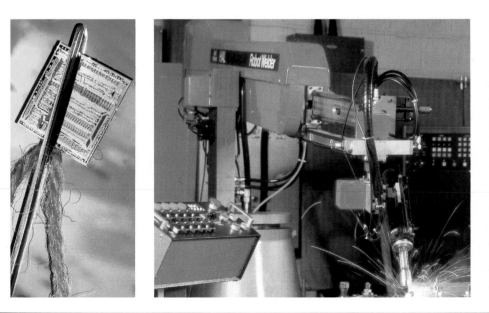

employed people to operate them. He thus pioneered the factory system of manufacturing.

In 1798 American inventor Eli Whitney demonstrated a revolutionary new method of manufacturing—the assembly of interchangeable parts. These are parts made so accurately by precision machine tools that they are virtually identical. Whitney showed how unskilled workers could quickly assemble a complicated product like a musket from a pile of parts. Hitherto only skilled gunsmiths had been able to make muskets, and very slowly.

NUMERICAL CONTROL

The assembly of interchangeable parts by relatively unskilled labour is still the basis of many modern manufacturing processes. And the key is still the use of precision machine tools to make precision parts.

These days many machine tools are automatic, or self-regulating. They position the workpiece, guide the cutting tool, reposition it and cut it again automatically. They work according to instructions fed to them in code on punched tape or magnetic tape. The code takes the form of numbers, and the method of operation is known as numerical control. Often several of these automatic machine tools work in unison, one performing a sequence of operations before handing over the workpiece to another.

Below: Similar robots can be programmed to carry out quite different tasks. The one on the left holds the stainless steel sink top in 200 different positions so that it can be polished all over. The robot on the right applies adhesive to car body parts.

Above: Man and machine combine to handle dangerous radioactive materials. The technician works a robot manipulator from outside the chamber containing the dangerous materials, using his hands to perform delicate movements.

ROBOTS

Car manufacturers have always been in the forefront of mechanization and mass-production from the beginning of the century, first with R.E. Olds (1901) and then Henry Ford (1908) pioneering car assembly on a production line.

Today on the car assembly line robots are as common as human workers. They are used specifically for welding and paint spraying, two tasks that human workers find unpleasant.

POLLUTION

The high technology of our modern world brings us a bewildering variety of benefits, but it also creates problems, particularly to the environment—our surroundings. For example, offshore oil wells supply much needed oil to power our vehicles and to provide essential raw materials for the chemical industry. But they are a potential environmental hazard. Periodically this is brought to our attention, as in June 1979 when a well blew out in the Gulf of Mexico and discharged oil into the sea at a prodigious rate. In two months an oil slick 650 km (400 miles) long had formed.

Oil slicks are one of the many forms of pollution, or poisoning of the environment, that is now occurring. Such pollution can threaten life—human as well as wildlife.

POLLUTION OF THE AIR

Motor vehicles are responsible for a great deal of the air pollution we suffer from. The petrol engine in particular produces poisonous fumes, including carbon monoxide, which is lethal even in minute quantities. It also produces gaseous lead compounds, and lead too is extremely toxic to human life because it accumulates in the body tissues.

Other major sources of air pollution are factories and conventional power stations that burn fossil fuels. Burning fuels produce a great deal of sulphur dioxide, an acidic gas that forms sulphuric acid in moist air. And when it rains, the rain is acid.

The effects of air pollution can be devastating. In certain climatic conditions, fumes and smoke get trapped by stagnant air in cities, such as Los Angeles, causing a choking smoky fog or smog. When acid rain falls, it eats away the stonework of buildings and corrodes any exposed metal. It acidifies lakes until they can no

longer support wildlife and it kills trees, often hundreds of kilometres from the source of the pollution. The lakes of Scandinavia and the forests of West Germany are already suffering catastrophically in this way.

WATER POLLUTION

Oil pollution has already been mentioned. It is already all too familiar on our beaches, soiling feet and clothes. More tragically the oil coats and kills seabirds and other seashore life. Inland waters do not escape, either. They can also be polluted by pesticides and fertilizers that run off farmland, and toxic effluents discharged from

chemical factories. Particularly harmful is the discharge of heavy metals such as cadmium and mercury. They can build up in the food chain—in fish and shellfish, for example—and poison birds and even human beings.

An even more insidious industrial discharge may escape into the environment from nuclear plants. It is waste that is radioactive. Doses of radiation can cause leukemia and cancers.

CONSERVATION

We are using up the Earth's resources at an alarming rate, producing and consuming billions of barrels of oil and billions of tonnes of ores every year. But these resources can only last so long. In

time the oil wells will run dry, the mines will become exhausted. And that time is not too far ahead, given our present rate of consumption. Oil and gas could run out early next century. So could gold, silver, platinum, copper, tin, zinc and lead. All these materials play a vital role in our technological age.

So we must try to conserve our precious resources as much as possible. We can do this in several ways. We can try to find substitutes for vital materials. This is being done, for example, in telecommunications, where glass fibres are replacing copper (see page 17). Another way to conserve is by recycling. Instead of committing our used cans and cars to the scrap heap, we must re-use the metal they contain.

Above: Massive construction projects like this hydroelectric dam in Siberia can lay waste vast areas of countryside and destroy the habitats of many animals and plants.

Top right: Recycling scrapped cars has now become big business.
Right: Scouts set up this dump in Florida to collect aluminium waste for recycling.

Left: An offshore oil platform ablaze in the Gulf of Mexico. Vast quantities of oil are escaping into the sea.

CHAPTER 6

CONSTRUC-TION

Uphill and down dale, across burning desert sands and icy wastes, in and under the oceans, construction engineers battle against the elements as they seek to change the face of the Earth for the benefit of mankind. They build high to eke out the precious space in our cities; they build long to span rivers and estuaries; they dig deep to tunnel through mountains; and they build massively to hold back mighty rivers.

The Thames Barrier, a unique construction project designed to prevent the city of London being flooded by exceptionally high tides. When danger threatens, cylindrical sections between the piers rotate and raise the flood gates into position.

BUILDINGS

To obtain protection from the weather and wild beasts, prehistoric people sought shelter in caves. They also made temporary shelters from branches. But surprisingly early they began building more permanent dwellings. There is evidence, near Nice in France, of a village of 21 huts with walls made of wooden stakes dating back 400,000 years!

However, building as we know it today began much more recently. The use of bricks dates from about 7000 BC. Hand-made mud bricks of this age have been found at the site of the ancient city of Jericho in the Middle East. As civilization progressed in that part of the world, people developed their building talents by constructing temples and monuments. By 3500 BC the Babylonians were building stepped pyramidal temples, called ziggurats, of bricks.

The ancient Egyptians later mastered the art of building in stone and constructed their magnificent pyramids. The oldest one standing is that at Sakkara, a stepped pyramid dating from about 2650 BC. But the biggest is the slightly later Great Pyramid of Khufu near Cairo. Built of over 2 million limestone blocks and orginally 146 metres (480 ft) tall, the pyramid weighs nearly 6 million tonnes. Astonishingly, it remained the world's most massive structure of any kind until the completion of dams like the Grand Coulee in the United States in the 1940s.

BUILDING HIGH

The Great Pyramid remained the world's highest structure for nearly 4000 years, until the great era of cathedral building began in Europe in the 1300s. In about 1307 the spire of Lincoln Cathedral in England soared to 160 metres (525 ft) high. The stone walls of the great cathedrals had to be very thick at the base in order to support the weight above.

Constructing ordinary buildings with such load-bearing walls is thus a great drawback, and restricts their height to about four or five storeys. Not until the 1880s did the solution to the problem become evident. In 1884 a Chicago architect designed a building with a rigid frame of cast and wrought iron and steel beams bolted together.

In the following year the 10-storey Home Insurance Building was completed. It was the first modern skyscraper, and provided the basic principle on which all skyscrapers have since been built. The metal frame, not the walls, carries the whole weight of the structure. The walls serve only to make the structure weatherproof. They can be built of light materials such as glass and aluminium panels. This type of construction, in which the walls simply hang on the frame, is known as curtain walling.

Today practically every modern city has its skyscraper blocks. Mostly they are office blocks or hotels. They are not used so widely for residential purposes because most people find that living in tall buildings is psychologically upsetting. Some skyscrapers are built for their prestige value to enchance the reputation of the company which builds them. But most are built for a sound practical reason. In most city centres where large businesses like to be there is little space at ground level for expansion. So the answer is to build upwards.

Pride of place among skyscrapers at present is the Sears Tower in Chicago. Its 100 storeys rise to a height of 443 metres (1454 ft), topping the next tallest building, the World Trade Center in New York City, by 28 metres (92 ft). The total floor area of the building is over 40 hectares (100 acres), one hundred times that of the plot on which it stands!

SKYSCRAPER CONSTRUCTION

Tall buildings cannot be built just anywhere. The properties of the soil at any site determines the height of the building that can be built there. The reason why Manhattan Island, New York City, has such a concentration of skyscrapers is that solid rock lies on or just beneath ground level. So it can form the base, or foundations of the buildings.

Other cities are not so fortunate,

Fact file . . .

A workforce of some 4000 people working for 30 years would have been needed to build the Great Pyramid.

The 102-storey, 300,000-tonne, 381-metre (1250-ft) tall Empire State Building was completed in 1930 after only 17 month's work. It is the 'fastest' skyscraper ever built.

Left: The exterior of many skyscrapers is just glass. The glass walls 'hang' from the rigid girder frame of the building, carrying no weight at all.

Right: Concrete dominates the design of the BMW Building in Munich, Germany.

Below: The 183-metre (600-ft) high National Westminster tower block under construction in London. The floors are built out from the central concrete core.

and firm foundations for the buildings must be constructed so that they don't sink under their weight or keel over. If the soil is reasonably firm, then a raft foundation can be used. This takes the form of a thick slab of concrete considerably wider than the building, so that the weight is spread over a larger area.

Where the soil is weak on top but stronger deeper down, a pile foundation must be used. This consists of a number of steel and reinforced-concrete columns, or piles, that are driven deep into the ground. Friction between the piles and the soil helps support the weight. A thick concrete slab is cast on top of the piles, and the building is built up on this.

The girders that form the skeleton of the building are put together storey by storey, being lifted into position by 'climbing' cranes, which are shifted upwards as the building rises. As soon as the girders are in place, work can start on constructing the floors and 'hanging' the walls. Work can proceed simultaneously on any floors since structurally speaking they are all independent. This makes for rapid construction.

The network of roads in Europe owes much to the ancient Romans, who were masterly construction engineers. After the fall of the Roman Empire however, the roads fell into disrepair. Not until the late 18th century was the art of roadbuilding revived by engineers like Thomas Telford and James Loudon McAdam. Their roads consisted of graded layers of crushed stones on a levelled base.

The loose-surfaced roads could not cope with the increasingly heavy motor traffic early this century and in particular threw up billowing clouds of dust. This was cured by mixing tar with the surface stones, producing tarmacadam, or tarmac, the same kind of mixture we use today for most roads.

Whereas the modern road system of Europe follows sinuous ancient routes, that of the United States was virtually purpose-built for the motor-car age. There was also more space available for road-building. So American roads are in general broad and straight. As befits the world's greatest car-owning country, the United States has the world's largest road network, which includes over 60,000 km (38,000 miles) of a superhighway known as the Interstate, which stretches from coast to coast.

PREPARING THE ROADBED

In the United States superhighways are often called expressways or freeways. Similar purpose-built roads have been built in most other countries too, where they are called such names as autobahn (Germany), autoroute (France) and motorway (Britain).

A motorway has separate carriageways carrying the traffic moving in different directions, and a barrier between the two. Other roads cross under or over the motorway. Traffic enters and leaves it at specially designed intersections which reduce the conflict between the traffic streams.

The route of a new motorway is

This highway network snakes through the centre of Miami, providing speedy access to all parts of the sprawling city. Carefully designed intersections allow traffic to leave and enter the main freeway without causing any disruption to through traffic. But congestion still occurs during the rush hours.

LAYING THE PAVEMENT

After the roadbed has been levelled, it is made firm, or compacted by heavy rollers. Now it is ready to receive the pavement, the name given to the actual structure of the road. This is made up of several layers. At the bottom, resting on the levelled soil, or subgrade, is a sub-base layer. This is usually made up of crushed stones or gravel. On top of this comes the roadbase.

For a concrete surface, a roadbase of lean (weak) concrete is used. On top of this is laid the surface concrete, to a depth of at least 25 cm (10 in) and more if the traffic is going to be heavy. Also for heavy-traffic roads, steel-mesh reinforcement is included in the surface layer. The construction of the concrete road is highly mechanized, being done by a succession of vehicles called a concrete train. It comprises a number of spreading and vibrating machines running along a set of guide rails, which are fed by ready-mixed concrete from mixer trucks.

The flexible tarmac surface is also laid by machines, which are fed with freshly made hot tarmac from a temporary plant set up nearby. The road is built up layer by layer, with each layer being compacted while still hot by heavy rollers.

Above: Developing the power of several hundred horses, a bulldozer clears the ground of rocks and rubble. Bulldozers blaze the trail for the other earthmoving machines.

Below: This self-propelled scraper moves prodigious loads of soil as it levels the road bed. It slices into the ground with a blade, rather like a woodworker's plane slices into wood.

Below right: Part of the train of vehicles that is involved in laying a concrete road.

first accurately surveyed, and then the giant earthmoving machines move in. Bulldozers remove obstructions such as tree stumps and rocks. They are powerful crawler-tracked vehicles with a curved blade in front which little can resist. Then come the scrapers to remove vast quantities of top soil. They are self-propelled machines with a box that has a scraper blade at the bottom. This slices into the soil as the scraper moves forward, and a layer of soil is scooped up into the box.

BRIDGES

From prehistoric times human beings have not liked getting their feet wet and have built bridges to avoid this. The earliest bridges consisted of tree trunks and slabs of stone resting on other stones. These simple bridges were what we call beam bridges. Such beam bridges can only span relatively small widths because the beams tend to sag in the middle.

Bridge-building remained primitive until about 2000 years ago when the Romans perfected the use of the arch. They built arch bridges of stone, and many still survive today. The bridges support their own weight and the load on them by transmitting it down the arch. Stone remained the sole material for arch bridges until 1779. In that year English ironmaster Abraham Darby built an arch bridge of iron at Coalbrookdale in Shropshire.

When in the middle of the 19th century steel became readily available, this became the prime bridge-building material. It led to such magnificent structures as the twin 520-metre (1700-ft) span Forth Rail Bridge (1890) in Scotland; the 503-metre (1650-ft) span Sydney Harbour Bridge (1932) in Australia; and the famous 1280-metre (4200-ft) span Golden Gate Bridge (1937) in San Francisco.

The Forth Rail Bridge was of cantilever design. A cantilever is a beam that is anchored one end and supported some way along so that the other end overhangs. A cantilever bridge consists of two such beams, whose overhangs meet in the middle. It is a design that allows quite a large span, but it is seldom used these days because of cheaper and better alternatives.

CABLE BRIDGES

The Golden Gate Bridge is yet another design, a suspension bridge. Its deck is suspended from a pair of firmly anchored cables that go up and over tall towers built near each end. Suspension bridges can span the largest gaps. The world's biggest is the Humber Bridge in north-east England, which has a span of 1410 metres (4630 ft).

Cable bridges of a different design are also becoming popular for bridging medium spans—from about 200–300 metres (656–984 ft). Known as cable-stayed bridges, they have one or more towers from which straight cables go down to the bridge deck. In the latest designs the towers are located on the centre line of the bridge. Many cable-stayed bridges are found in Germany, where the design originated. They include the elegant Severins Bridge at Cologne and the Friedrich Ebert Bridge at Bonn, both over the River Rhine.

Today's bridges are such large structures that designers have to allow for the effects of the wind on them. They usually test scale models of their designs in wind tunnels to see how they behave.

Right: Stages in the construction of the world's longest-span bridge, the Humber Bridge in north-east England. The four inset pictures show activities common to all suspension-bridge building. They are: (1) Building up the suspension towers from the river bed. (2) Spinning the suspension cables from steel wires. (3) The twin suspension cables completed. (4) Lifting the bridge deck into position.

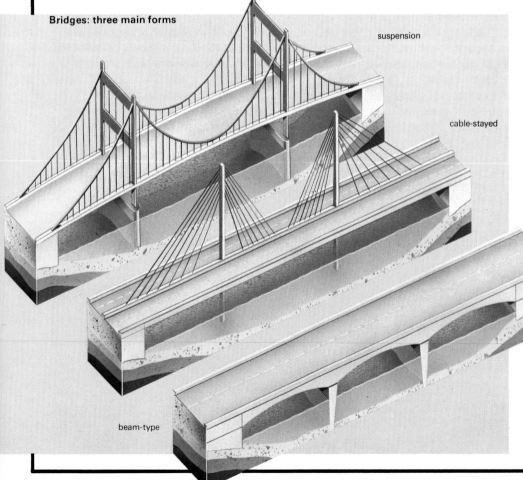

Bridges: three main forms

suspension

cable-stayed

beam-type

Left: Three types of bridges widely used today. Simplest is the beam bridge, which requires supporting piers at regular intervals. Of the two cable-bridge designs, the suspension bridge can span by far the biggest gaps.

BRIDGE-BUILDING

The foremost materials for constructing bridges these days are concrete and steel, often combined in the form of reinforced concrete, strengthened with rods or wires of steel. The steel imparts tensile or stretching strength, which adds to the compressive strength of the concrete to make an ideal constructional material.

Reinforced-concrete construction is used in bridges of many kinds. It makes possible particularly elegant arch bridges like the Gladesville Bridge in Sydney, which has a span of 300 metres (984 ft). The arch is formed from pre-cast segments, assembled over supporting framework. When they are all in place, the framework is removed and the arch supports the load.

Steel is used in vast quantities in suspension bridges for the bridge deck, usually for the suspension towers, and for the cables from which the deck is suspended. The cables are composed of thousands of high-tensile steel wires. In the Humber Bridge, for example, there are nearly 15,000 of them, galvanized (coated with zinc) for corrosion protection. The steel bridge deck of the Humber Bridge is of shallow box section, streamlined so as to create as little wind drag as possible.

Steel box-section, or box-girder construction is now used for many bridges, including the magnificent Europa Bridge near Innsbruck in Austria, which rises more than 160 metres (525 ft) above the valley bottom. Box-girder bridges typically consist of a concrete roadway carried on one or two steel box sections, stiffened inside by stringers to help prevent buckling.

The box sections are usually cantilevered out from the supporting piers. Sometimes reinforced-concrete box sections are used instead, in which case they are often erected from overhead scaffolding and stuck in place by powerful epoxy resin adhesives.

DAMS

Beavers like to build their lodge (home) in a stream so that its entrance is under water. If they find that the water level in the stream is too low, they construct a dam across it, using tree trunks, branches, mud and stones. The water level behind the dam rises and the beavers are happy. Human engineers beaver away too, damming rivers to raise water levels. They may do this for various reasons—to prevent flooding, to store water for irrigation, to improve navigation, and to produce power.

Irrigation dams are particularly important in hot countries that have a wet season and a dry season. In the wet season the rain falls torrentially, the rivers swell and flood, often with devastating consequences and loss of life. In the dry season the rivers start to dry up and the surrounding countryside is starved of water. So the idea of the dam is to collect the water from the rainy season and then release it gradually throughout the dry season. The Tarbela Dam across the River Indus in Pakistan is a dam of this kind. One of the world's biggest dams, it is 2.7 km (1.7 miles) long, 150 metres (492 ft) high and has a volume of 190 million cubic metres (145 million cubic yards).

Among the dams that have been built to produce hydroelectric power, none is more productive than the Grand Coulee Dam on the Columbia River in Washington State, USA. Completed as long ago as 1942, it can generate up to 10,000 megawatts of electricity.

UNUSUAL DAMS

In Brittany, France, the River Rance is dammed across its estuary in an

The crest of the Grande Dixence dam in Switzerland, the world's tallest dam. Rising some 285 metres (935 ft) above the valley floor, it is a gravity dam constructed from a million tonnes of concrete.

unusual hydroelectric scheme. It produces power from the rise and fall of the tides. A much bigger sea dam has been built across the entrance to the Zuiderzee in the Netherlands to prevent flooding of the reclaimed lowland areas. Called the Afsluitdijk, it stretches for over 30 km (20 miles).

A movable dam across the River Thames at Woolwich, called the Thames Barrier (see picture, page 90), has been built to prevent possible flooding of London by exceptionally high tides. The flood gates can be raised quickly when danger threatens.

GRAVITY DAMS

The Tarbela and the Grand Coulee dams mentioned above are both massive structures whose sheer weight keeps them in place. They are known as gravity dams. But they are made up of different materials and are constructed differently— one uses earth, rock and clay, the other uses concrete.

The Tarbela Dam is a type called an earth-fill, or embankment dam. This kind of dam is constructed simply by dumping truck loads of soil and rocks in position. Usually it is given a core of clay or similar material to make it watertight. The core will extend down some way into the ground so as to prevent seepage of water underneath. The final dam will be very broad at the base and then slope inwards on both sides towards the top.

The 167-metre (550 ft) high Grand Coulee Dam has quite a different profile. Like most concrete gravity dams, it is more or less triangular in cross-section, with the face against the water being upright. It is thickest at the base, where it experiences the greatest water pressure—something like 20 kg per sq cm (290 lb per sq inch). Its total weight is nearly 20 million tonnes, making it the biggest concrete structure in the world.

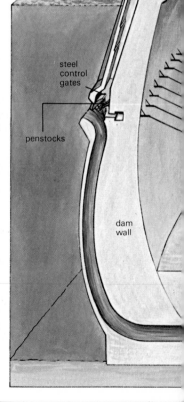

reservoir

air vents to penstocks

steel control gates

penstocks

dam wall

ARCH DAMS

The illustration below of the Reza Shah Kabir Dam shows another kind of dam. It is also made of concrete but is very much thinner than the gravity dam. This is because it relies not upon its weight to withstand the water pressure, but upon its shape. It curves in the shape of an arch, with the curve pointing towards the water. And it is known as an arch dam.

Above: The Reza Shah Kabir dam in Iran is an arch dam built across a narrow gorge. It is some 185 metres (600 ft) tall. Its curved shape gives it its strength.

Left: A sideways view of the dam, showing how the water from the reservoir is piped into the turbines in the power house. They spin generators to produce electricity.

roadway

spillway channels

power house

generator

turbine inlet

turbine

TUNNELS & PIPELINES

Construction engineers not only work on and above the ground, they also work beneath it, digging tunnels to reach mineral deposits in mines; to carry water in water-supply schemes; to carry underground railways beneath the congested roads of our cities; to carry roads and railways through the mountains or under the sea so as to avoid a lengthy detour.

The era of modern tunnelling began in the late 1800s when the first great rail tunnels were driven through the Alps in Europe. Magnificent tunnels are still being driven through the Alps today. One of the latest is the St Gotthard (completed 1980), at 16 km (10 miles) long, the world's longest road tunnel.

The Japanese have also been in the forefront of tunnelling technology in recent years, completing in 1985 the 54-km (33-mile) Seikan tunnel 100 metres (330 ft) below the seabed of Tsugaru

Strait. In the early 1990s a tunnel under the English Channel only a few kilometres shorter will link England and France by rail for the first time. The Channel tunnel, or Chunnel, will extend from Cheriton near Folkestone to Frethun near Calais, heading through chalk rock some 40 metres (130 ft) beneath the seabed.

TUNNELLING METHODS

The simplest method of tunnelling is used when the tunnel need only be just below the surface. Known as cut-and-cover, this method has been widely used over the years for building tunnels for underground railways such as much of the London Underground and the Paris Métro. A huge trench is excavated from ground level ('cut') and then the tunnel is roofed over ('cover').

This method, however, has limited use, and most tunnels have to be driven much deeper

Above: This is a jumbo drilling rig, which is used to drill shot holes in the rock face during tunnelling.

Top right: Work proceeding on the Trans-Alaskan Pipeline in the far north of Alaska.

Left: A full-face tunnelling machine that can bore through solid rock. The cutters (red) grind away the rock as the head rotates.

underground. They may be excavated with the help of explosives or by machines, which are often called 'moles'. The basic technique of tunnelling through hard rock with explosives has changed little over the years. Holes are drilled in the rock face with compressed-air, or electro-hydraulic drills. Dynamite is placed in the holes and exploded. The broken up rock, or spoil, is then removed, and the process starts all over again. This process is mechanized today by having a number of drills mounted on hydraulic booms on a mobile platform, or 'jumbo'. The jumbo can drill many holes simultaneously.

THE MECHANICAL MOLES

The machines used for tunnelling through hard rock are often called

full-facers. They have a cutting head studded with a set of hardened-steel disc cutters (see picture, left). When the head rotates, the cutters revolve and grind their way through the rock. One set of hydraulic rams pushes sideways against the tunnel walls, providing the grip, while another set drives the cutting head.

Behind the cutting head is the control cabin where workers operate the machine. They work inside a cylindrical shield that protects them against possible cave-ins. The spoil is carried back to the rear of the machine by a belt conveyor and feeds into rail wagons. Another hydraulic-ram mechanism forces concrete or steel segments into place to form the tunnel lining.

In machines for tunnelling through soft and waterlogged ground pressure must be applied to prevent the water and soft soil

flowing in. This is done traditionally by means of a pressurized tunnelling shield, in which the operators work. But in the latest machines only the cutting head is pressurized, and it is pressurized with a fluid clay called bentonite, not air.

PIPELINES

The lengthiest underground construction projects, however, are not tunnels but pipelines. Pipelines are used on a vast scale to transport oil and natural gas in particular.

Pipeline laying is in general not technically difficult. It simply involves welding lengths of steel pipe together, burying them in an excavated trench, and covering them over. The biggest challenges pipeline engineers face are coping with the terrain along the pipeline route and with the weather.

CHAPTER 7

MEDICINE

Using tailor-made drugs and the most intricate surgical techniques, doctor and surgeon can mend the diseased and damaged human body as never before. Ingenious scanning machines help their diagnosis, while other machines provide vital life-support functions for the body. Transplanted organs promise gravely ill patients a new lease of life, as do artificial 'spare parts' for malformed and damaged limbs and organs.

The body scanner has become a powerful tool for examining internal organs and tissues. A beam of X-rays is passed from different directions through a thin 'slice' of the body. A computer builds up an internal picture of this body slice and displays it on a video screen on the control console.

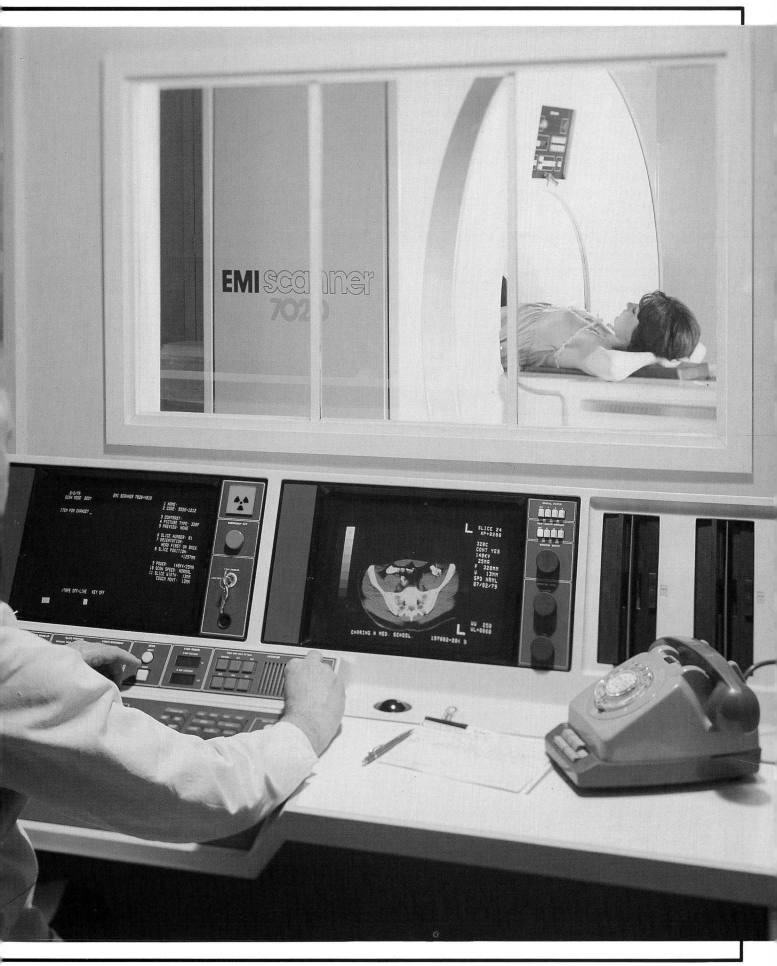

BEATING DISEASE

The human race, the most advanced life form on Earth, is frequently laid low and often killed by some of the lowliest organisms—viruses and bacteria. Such microscopic organisms cause diseases: everything from the common cold to dysentry, from blood poisoning to smallpox, from malaria to cancer. Somehow they overcome the body's natural defence mechanisms. Human beings, like all animals, experience pain when they hurt themselves or suffer from diseases. And some of their body organs may not work as well as they should.

This has always been so since the dawn of civilization, and for an equally long time human beings have tried to do something about it. Over the years they discovered that certain diseases or conditions could be combatted by eating or drinking substances obtained from plants. Extracts from the opium poppy would take away pain; extracts from foxgloves would relieve certain heart conditions; chewing the bark of the cinchona tree would fight malaria. These natural substances that helped the body fight pain and infection were among the first drugs.

SYNTHETIC DRUGS

In the great flowering of chemistry in the 19th century, chemists began analysing the natural plant drugs to find the active ingredients. Eventually they isolated digitalis

Right: An experimental unit for producing interferon (inset below). This is a powerful drug that protects the body from attack by many viruses and some cancers. At present interferon is difficult and expensive to manufacture.

from the foxglove; quinine from cinchona bark; and morphine from the opium poppy. Not only did they isolate these drugs, they also found ways of making them synthetically. The same happened with the drug insulin, a hormone drug originally obtained from the pancreas of sheep. Synthesis meant that the drugs became available in sufficient quantities to treat everyone who needed them.

Entirely new drugs were also produced which had no natural counterpart. Most familiar is aspirin, which is the chemical acetylsalicylic acid. Originally obtained from coal tar, it was and is very widely used as an analgesic, or painkiller. Outstanding among the other synthetic drugs are the sulphonamides, or sulpha drugs, discovered in the 1930s. They combat deadly diseases such as pneumonia and meningitis.

These days researchers try to 'design' drugs with specific treatments in mind, using their knowledge of the action of certain chemical groups on organisms. One of the first of these tailor-made drugs was cimetidine, which is used specifically for treating peptic ulcers.

Fact file . . .

Since the 5th century AD, the life expectancy for Britons has increased from 33 (male) and 27 (female), to the present 71 (male) and 77 (female).

A liquid fluorocarbon emulsion called fluosol can carry oxygen around the body, just like blood.

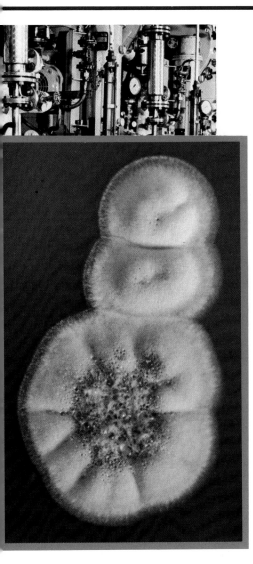

Some of the humblest living things produce a range of drugs that combat disease. They include the moulds from which we get penicillin (above).

ANTIBIOTICS

The most widely used group of drugs prescribed these days, however, are not synthetic but are produced by certain moulds, they are the antibiotics. They are produced by growing the moulds in a suitable nutrient, or culture medium. The original one, which is still very important, was penicillin. The British chemist Alexander Fleming discovered penicillin in 1928, but its medicinal properties were not fully appreciated until 10 years later. Over the years penicillin has been joined by many more antibiotics, obtained from

different moulds or fungi. They include streptomycin, tetracycline, chloromycetin and terramycin.

Some moulds produce compounds that have other useful actions. Cyclosporin is such a compound. It is a drug that is now widely used to prevent the body rejecting organ transplants (see page 108). Since its use began in 1978, the success of kidney transplants, for example, has improved from about 50 per cent to 80 per cent.

HELPING THE BODY'S DEFENCES

Vaccinating is another invaluable method of combatting disease. Vaccines consist of dead or weakened germs. They work by stimulating the body's natural defences to produce antibodies against the germs. So when the body is afterwards exposed to the germs, the antibodies kill them before they can multiply and do any real harm. Edward Jenner produced the first vaccine, against smallpox, in 1796. Once one of the biggest killers, smallpox has now been eradicated throughout the

world by mass vaccinations. Vaccinations are now widely available for other diseases.

Other ways of marshalling the body's defences are also being found. They include treatment with substances released naturally when the body cells are attacked. One is called interferon. It is produced when cells are attacked by viruses and prevents them attacking other cells.

The treatment of many virus infections by interferon has been successful, and there is evidence that certain cancers may be treatable too. The main problem with interferon is that it is difficult and expensive to produce in large quantities. Some increase in production has been achieved by using genetic engineering methods. Genes that control the production of interferon are introduced into bacteria such as *E. Coli*, which are then cultured on a large scale and produce the drug themselves.

Below: Drugs used in large quantities, such as aspirin, are produced in automated chemical factories under carefully controlled conditions.

MEDICAL MACHINES

The increasing use of machines over the years has brought about striking advances in medicine. The machines are used both for diagnosis—determining what is wrong—for treatment, and for monitoring body activity.

Some machines have been available for many years, including the electroencephalograph (EEC) and electrocardiograph (ECG). These measure, respectively, the electrical rhythms of the brain and the heart. Erratic EEC or ECG readouts can indicate brain and heart disorders.

X-ray machines are also standard equipment in hospitals, and also dentists' surgeries. They work by passing invisible and highly penetrating X-rays through the body and recording what comes through on a photographic plate. The rays pass readily through the soft body tissues but are partly blocked by the bones. So on the photographic plate the bones stand out, and any break or fracture in them can be seen. Pictures of the digestive tract can also be obtained by having the patient consume a 'barium meal'. This is a white liquid that contains barium sulphate, which blocks X-rays.

Below: A pregnant woman having an ultrasonic scan. The machine uses sound echoes to build up a picture of the unborn baby in the womb, which is displayed on the monitor screen.

Machines come to the aid of premature babies. They are kept under ideal conditions in incubators and sometimes put on a ventilator (inset) to assist breathing.

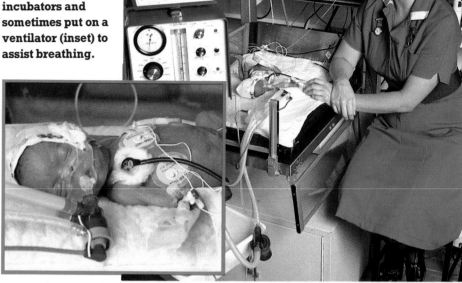

THE SCANNERS

The soft tissues of the body organs do not show up well in an ordinary X-ray picture. But a relatively new X-ray machine (1973) produces a very detailed picture of the internal organs. It is known as a computerized tomographic (CT) scanner. 'Tomography' means something like 'studying a slice'. And the CT machine does examine a thin slice of the body by projecting a beam of X-ray through it from different directions. A series of detectors records the strength of the rays passing through, and the results go into a computer.

From the results, the computer creates a picture of the body slice that shows up everything—tissues as well as bones. Any growths or other abnormalities present can be spotted. The technique can be applied to every part of the body, including the brain. It has completely revolutionized the diagnosis of brain disorders.

Two experimental scanners also use similar computerized techniques, but not with X-rays. One is called PET (positron emission tomography). The patient inhales slightly radioactive oxygen, which passes into the brain. Scans reveal what parts of the brain are involved in various activities, such as vision. The technique of NMR (nuclear magnetic resonance) involves applying a strong magnetic field, and detecting the slight radiation the atoms of the brain give out when the field is removed.

Future scanners will probably use non X-ray techniques.

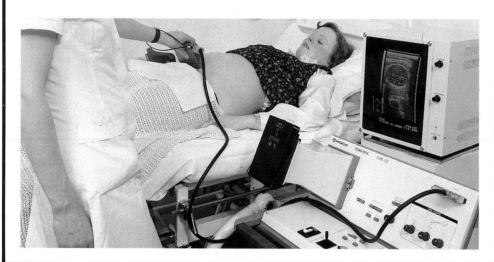

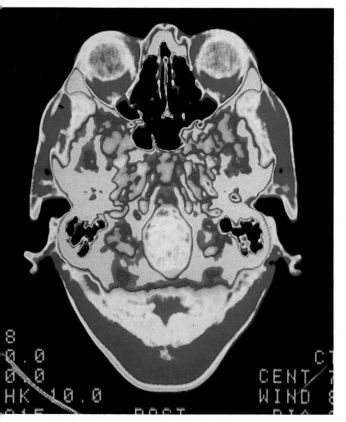

Left: A multicoloured image of a cross-section of the human brain. It was made by computer processing the data from a scanning X-ray machine.

Below: This patient is about to undergo radiotherapy— treatment by radiation. Radiotherapy is widely used for treating tumours before they invade the whole body.

waste products such as urea build up in your blood and will eventually poison you. So two or three times a week, for a minimum of about 30 hours, kidney sufferers have to undergo dialysis on a machine often called an artifical kidney. In this machine the patient's blood is pumped past a membrane which allows the waste products to pass out. The standard kidney machine is room-sized, but successful suitcase-size machines are now becoming available.

SURGICAL LASERS

Lasers produce a very intense beam of pure light, which can be focused to produce very high temperatures. Industrially they are used for cutting metals, but in medicine they can be used to cut and puncture human tissue. Some surgeons now use laser scalpels. They cut very precisely and also prevent undue bleeding by cauterizing, or heat-sealing the blood vessels.

In eye surgery lasers are used to 'weld' back in place retinas that have become detached. They are also being widely used to treat glaucoma, a condition in which pressure builds up in the eye. The laser beam punches a tiny hole through the cornea of the eye to relieve the pressure.

SOUNDS GOOD

Another type of scanner is now widely used for checking the well-being of unborn babies. But it uses sound waves, not X-rays, which in large doses could harm the babies. The machine uses the same technique ships use to detect submarines and bats use to navigate. It is sonar, or sound echo location. The sonar scanner uses a probe that emits sound waves beyond the range of the human ear. They are ultrasonic.

In a sonar scan, the doctor moves the probe over the abdomen of the pregnant woman. The sound waves are reflected by the internal body tissues and those of the baby, and picked up by the probe as echoes. The echoes are then displayed as a scan on a monitor screen. The scan shows up the outline of the baby and can indicate, for example, whether the umbilical cord is in the right place for delivery.

A number of machines have been developed to take over the function of body organs when they fail or are

otherwise out of order, for example, during operations. Heart transplants and open-heart surgery, for instance, would be impossible without the heart-lung machine, which pumps blood around the body and replenishes it with oxygen.

Most people with diseased or absent kidneys would not be alive were it not for the kidney machine. When your kidneys do not work,

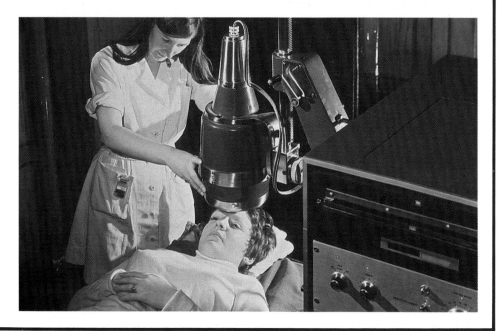

MAKING & MENDING

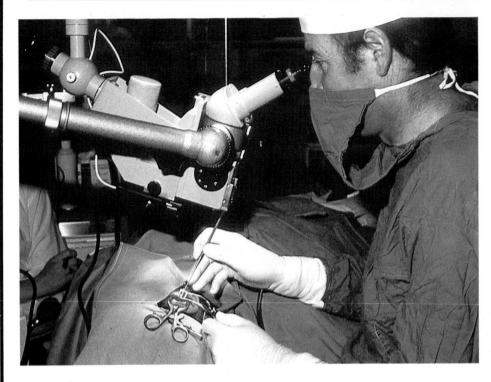

Left: Surgeons as well as research scientists now use microscopes in their work. They use microscopes when performing intricate operations, such as joining fine blood vessels and nerves.

Below: An artificial heart pacemaker, which is powered by a nuclear battery. It has a long life and can be implanted into the chest cavity.

Along with the great improvements in treating diseases by drugs and machines in recent years have come astonishing advances in surgical medicine. Surgeons these days not only cut things off and take things out, they can also stick things back on or replace them. The three main areas of surgery involved are microsurgery, transplants and spare-part surgery.

MICROSURGERY

In microsurgery, the surgeon performs intricate operations looking through a microscope. They typically involve the joining together of tiny blood vessels and nerves too fine to be handled by conventional surgical techniques. The surgeon works with the finest of instruments, with scalpels little bigger than a pin and needles not much thicker than an eyelash.

Microsurgery has been particularly effective in replacing severed limbs and fingers. As long as the injury is a clean one and the limb is not crushed, then there is a good chance of saving it. But time is of the essence because the severed limb will quite quickly become

irreversibly damaged and will not 'take'. It can take anything up to 12 hours to replace a severed limb.

Another field where microsurgery is proving invaluable is in some forms of deep skin grafting. Patches of skin with blood vessels attached can now be transferred from one site to another and connected to the blood vessels there. The previous techniques required a whole series of operations that took months.

TRANSPLANTING ORGANS

Not so long ago if you had severely diseased kidneys and had them removed, you would have to spend many hours a week on a dialysis machine. Today you stand a chance of leading a normal life again by having a kidney transplant. Someone else's kidney would be removed and placed in your body. The heart, the liver and the lungs are other body organs that can also now be transplanted. But they do not have the same success rate as kidneys.

The main problem with transplanting someone else's organs into your body is rejection.

The body's natural immune, or protective system tries to fight against the new tissue, which it rightly regards as 'foreign' and potentially dangerous. The new tissue becomes inflamed and eventually dies.

Great pains are therefore taken to prevent rejection. One method of reducing the risk is by carrying out tissue typing. This means trying to get a good match between the type of body tissues of a potential donor and the patient. In the case of kidney transplants, a close relative of the patient may produce an excellent tissue match, and can donate one of his or her kidneys for transplanting. This is possible because a person can live perfectly well with only one kidney.

Rejection is also treated by drugs which reduce the body's reaction to foreign tissues. Certain compounds similar to the hormone drug cortisone have this effect, but unfortunately also reduce the body's defences against other

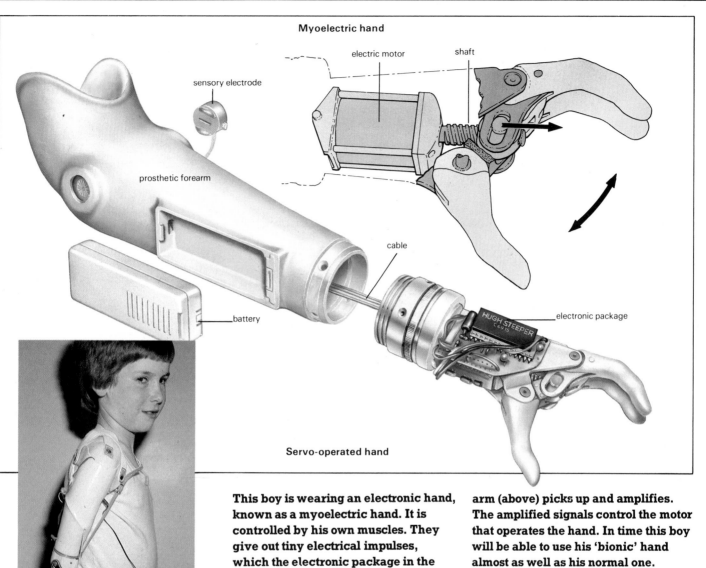

Myoelectric hand

electric motor   shaft

sensory electrode

prosthetic forearm

cable

battery

electronic package

HUGH STEEPER
C-6975

Servo-operated hand

infections. Other drugs, such as Cyclosporin, seem to work better. They prevent rejection without reducing the body's resistance to other infections.

SPARE-PART MEDICINE

For centuries people have used artificial limbs, such as wooden legs, to replace those severed by accident or disease, as they do today. False teeth and glass eyes

This boy is wearing an electronic hand, known as a myoelectric hand. It is controlled by his own muscles. They give out tiny electrical impulses, which the electronic package in the arm (above) picks up and amplifies. The amplified signals control the motor that operates the hand. In time this boy will be able to use his 'bionic' hand almost as well as his normal one.

have also been with us for a long time. Such artificial body parts are called prostheses.

Modern prostheses can be very sophisticated indeed. The pictures above show an electronically controlled artificial hand, often called a bionic ('biological electronic') hand. It is driven by a battery-powered electric motor. But the clever thing about it is that it is controlled by the body muscles that would normally have controlled the original arm. Muscles work by generating tiny electrical impulses, and in the bionic arm these impulses are amplified by electronics to control the electric motor that operates the hand.

However, the biggest advance in this branch of medicine is spare-part surgery. Artificial parts are now

routinely implanted in the body to replace those that are malformed or diseased. Damaged heart valves are replaced with ones made of plastic. Diseased arteries and veins are replaced by plastic and silicone rubber tubes. The plastics used include polyurethane, Dacron and Teflon, which are highly inert materials that do not react with, or irritate the body tissues.

Experiments are also taking place with implanting complete artificial hearts. The most successful has been the Jarvik-7, developed at the University of Utah in Salt Lake City, USA. Made of aluminium and polyurethane and powered by compressed air, such hearts have managed to keep people alive for months at a time—a real medical miracle.

INDEX

Picture credits